Gui

BOOK OF
Amazing
Dog Tales

Edited by
NEIL EWART

RINGPRESS

Foreword

Robert Killick

The presence of dogs in the lives of human beings is little short of miraculous. They constantly find new ways of worming their way into our hearts. Quite why the dog is the only species of animal that has concerned itself with humans is a mystery that will never be solved.

Apart from the companionship and the uncompromising love they give to every pet owner, dogs serve us in innumerable ways – as Guide Dogs for the Blind, Hearing Dogs for the Deaf, Dogs for the Disabled, Search and Rescue Dogs, police dogs... the list goes on. We all have much for which we should be grateful.

Neil Ewart, who collected these stories, is a dyed-in-the-wool dog man. He understands dogs, and his profound knowledge of guide dogs, built up over many years, serves him in good stead when it comes to assessing stories of both dogs and people, with all their quirks and peculiarities.

I know Neil well. He has devoted his life to the service of dogs, and he feels that if this book helps in the understanding and appreciation of what dogs are, and what they can do for mankind, he will have succeeded.

© Ringpress Books & Neil Ewart 2003

First published in 2003 by Ringpress Books a division of
Interpet Publishing, Vincent Lane, Dorking, Surrey RH4 3YX United Kingdom

British Library Cataloguing in Publication Data
A CIP record for this book is available from the British Library

ISBN 1 86054 214 X

Cartoons: Russell Jones

Introduction

Neil Ewart

There is nothing original in writing to a number of people and asking them for contributions to a book of anecdotes. However, I have deliberately decided to avoid approaching celebrities, politicians and others that are normally expected to make contributions. This is not to be disparaging to such persons, but I wanted to get together some memories from people who have had direct dealings with Guide Dogs over the years and whom I would count amongst our many friends.

I have always admired those who actually 'do' something with dogs and can genuinely claim to have a wealth of experience.

On behalf of Guide Dogs, I must thank all those individuals and other organisations who have willingly contributed. All were asked to provide stories that could be funny or sad. The only stipulation was that they must be true!

Some are short, others much longer. Which you read will depend on how tired you are!

Put a pint pot in any dog owner's hand and the stories will flow. There is obviously scope for a whole series of similar books. If you are reading this in a bookshop and wondering whether to make a purchase, do not hesitate. If enough are sold then, perhaps, there may be a second volume... more stories will be sought and one of them might be from you!

Royalties from the sale of this book will go towards the work of Guide Dogs for the Blind.

Guardian Angels

Mike Mullan, dog trainer and Kennel Club member

Her name was Ribs. We acquired her when she was about five years old from a pub in Kent where she had been most of her life. The publican and his wife called her Ribs because, when they had found her abandoned at around six months, they could see every bone in her body. When we got her, she was the complete opposite, having been grossly over-fed. She needed a few months to transform into a super-fit, really good-looking Dobe, who could enjoy life to the full.

Ribs formed a great bond with my daughter, Delia, who was then three years old. Everywhere Delia went, Ribs would go too. She really was a big softie, never showing any signs of aggression. If the doorbell rang, she would bark but was never threatening.

However, this was not the case when, on a late-summer afternoon walk with my wife, Moira, and our crossbred Dobe, Bruno, Ribs sensed that all was not well. Events proved later that, perhaps, true guarding instincts really are part of the Dobermann nature.

Moira always walked the dogs on a piece of land called Frimley Fuel Allotments, consisting of some 300 acres of heath and woodland, which is open to the public. On that particular day, Moira noticed a man in a tracksuit running towards her and the dogs. She immediately called the pair back to her, but they would only come to within 20 yards of her and then turned to face the man, who was still rapidly approaching. With the two dogs ahead and each to the side of her, Moira called again and again, but both stood their ground.

We have always prided ourselves on our dogs' recall and Moira became concerned that there could be an

accident. She called to the runner to stop to give her a
chance to get the dogs in.

The request was met with a torrent of abuse and again
Moira made the same request. The runner yelled more
abuse while still heading towards her. There was no
reason why he could not choose a totally different
direction to pass her, as there were no obstacles in sight.

Once he was about 30 yards away, Ribs decided
enough was enough and the man was definitely bad
news. So, in she went, knocking him to the ground. She
stood over him, teeth bared, her back up and snarling as
only an angry Dobe can, but not actually biting him.
Moira was now thoroughly alarmed, not only for her

safety but for that of the floored victim.

Once more, Moira called Ribs and was relieved when she did return. However, she still would not come right to her side, as she would normally do. She stood firmly between Moira and the runner.

He regained his feet and although white-faced and shaking, he continued to offer abuse and accused Ribs of biting him on the left leg. A composed Moira quickly pointed out that if Ribs had really bitten him, he would not be standing on the injured leg.

By now, Bruno had got the idea, and although the dogs were close to Moira, both were ready and willing to pitch in if the runner was fool enough to provoke more trouble.

Well, that was the end of the incident and fortunately Moira had not been physically injured in any way.

Later that day, we decided to report the incident to the local police. They were curious that the runner had not contacted them; however, they asked for a statement in case he should.

During the statement, Moira was asked for a description of the man. The police attitude changed as soon as she gave one, and two CID officers were called in. They requested that Moira went over the description in detail.

Moira's description accurately matched that of a man they were looking for in connection with a previous incident that had occurred a couple of miles way, involving a lady walking her two Labradors.

She had been attacked and murdered!

The whole incident really brought home to me how the natural instincts in the dog can come to the fore when it really matters. Ribs never showed that side of her nature again – that is, not until two years later when... ah, but that's another story, isn't it?

Highly Stung

Jenny Moir, head of PR, Hearing Dogs For Deaf People

When Roddy, a Papillon, was in training, he got stung by a wasp and had a really bad reaction to it – so bad that he was rushed to the vet's. Luckily, he recovered,

completed his training, and went to a recipient called Doreen. A couple of weeks after Roddy had been placed with Doreen, he went and scrabbled at her. When she asked "What is it?", he led her to his bed, where she saw a wasp. He moved back until she had got rid of it, then went and lay in his bed and fell sleep!

Something Different 1

Hugh Hawkins, vet

Leaning over a gate with the farmer, I reliably informed him that I didn't think the poorly animal would make it. On cue, the cow took a large breath and fell over dead. The farmer turned and congratulated me on the accuracy of my diagnosis.

Dial M For Murder

Tom Buckley, General Secretary of the British Institute of Professional Dog Trainers

My true story is set in 1951. My business partner and I had started the first security company specialising in the use of patrol dogs some three years earlier. As little was known about the value of dogs in this role, business was not exactly brisk. In fact, we had to augment our income by private training, a demonstration team and working as relief guards on the few sites that we had.

We once had an enquiry from a Mrs Samuels of Manchester asking us to train Rover, her 12-month-old German Shepherd, as a companion and guard. When I called to see the dog, a well-boned, ginger-coloured specimen with a super temperament, I was told that Mr Samuels was at work. He would have liked to have met me, but he was leaving all arrangements to his wife. Having quoted an approximate price, plus hand-over tuition for both husband and wife, and subsequent additional visits if required, Rover and I went merrily on our way.

I have never had such pleasure out of training a dog as I did with Rover. He was an absolute dream and only needed showing an exercise a couple of times to be near perfect. His wish to please knew no bounds.

I returned him to his owners after the agreed three weeks and they were delighted with the results. They became interested in dog training, and formed a local club.

I became quite friendly with the Samuels and would board Rover for them when they went away. They were an extremely courteous couple and I never sensed anything to be wrong in any way.

Time passed, about 12 months or so, when I arrived home from a night duty to be asked by my wife, Margaret, if I had been trying to phone her. Apparently, Margaret had been awakened at 6am and 7.30am, and on both occasions the phone had stopped ringing before she could get downstairs and answer it.

I arrived home just after 8am, and we racked our brains to think who might have been trying to reach us. Curious about these mystery calls, we telephoned all the people we thought might be trying to get in touch. No one had. The next morning's newspapers gave the answer.

The headline said: "Wife stabbed to death: husband kills himself."

The husband was an Albert Samuels. I recognised the name immediately, and, after the initial shock and sadness, my thoughts were focused on what had happened to Rover while all this was going on, and where he was now.

I jumped into the car and sped off, as fast as my 1938 Morris Eight Saloon would go, to the Samuels' house. Detectives at the scene welcomed me with open arms, as they said that a German Shepherd had gone berserk and no one had been able to get near it. I went to the rear of the house, calling the dog's name, and trying to whistle through dried-up lips. Well, I didn't know if he had gone bonkers or not. Outside a crowd anxiously watched. A newspaper of the time reported the following:

"Rover faced Tom with his eyes red, and black nostrils dilated, his hair ragged, his lips drawn back from his teeth. Then he sprang!

For a second, Tom felt a nervous flutter in his stomach as the dog hurled itself at him. A paw hit him in the chest. Suddenly Rover's tongue was licking his face in mad happiness".

It was something like that but the reporter did excel himself.

The murder had taken place at 1am and police enquiries revealed that Mr Samuels did make two attempts to call from a telephone box near his house. An inquest report stated:

"Samuels left a letter saying his mind was sound and not disturbed. The letter ended with a request that someone look after his dog and with a plea that God would have mercy on his soul".

The murderer in this narrative came over to this country from the West Indies during the war and served as a physical education instructor in the Royal Air Force. He was also a pretty good boxer and had been employed as a sparring partner for the Turpin brothers. In fact, he forecast the rise to fame of Randolph, the younger brother, who was not a well-known name at the time.

In 1951, murder was a hanging offence. Before committing suicide, Mr Samuels risked being caught and executed for the sake of his dog's well-being.

I often wonder what Mr Samuels would have said to me if I had been there to answer the telephone.

Fido Foodies

Brigadier John Clifford, Royal Army
Veterinary Corps (retired)

Sally the Springer Spaniel was a rescue dog, and, although we never knew her full history, it was obvious she hadn't had a good time of it. Outside, she was sure-footed, brave and full of adventure; however, in the house, the smallest movement or unexpected sound could stress her for hours. She loved to be with us, but too many people in one room would send her scuttling into her kennel or under the bed.

We had Sally for 13 wonderful years, and although all dogs are full of character, Sally's was all the more appealing because she did the unexpected.

It was a regular summer Saturday afternoon in our newsagent's shop – not much happening, but plenty of ice-cream sales. The phone rang, and the hairdresser from four shops along said two of her clients had noticed a black-and-white Springer Spaniel peering at them over the parapet of the shop front. Was it ours?

I ran up to the bedroom and Sally was nowhere in sight. I glanced at the open window and thought there was no way she could have fitted through it. I double-checked, and, sure enough, Sally was running back and forth along the tiny ledge overhanging the shop fronts, pausing only to peer over if anyone interesting went in or out of the shops.

I called her, and she seemed pleased to see me – so pleased, in fact, she came flying towards me and leapt through the open window, without even pausing – the gap was about 18 inches square.

Sally never got out of the habit of scavenging for food and several times stole grub most unsuitable for a dog. The day we moved into our first flat, my parents helped us to move, and we left all the dogs (their two dogs plus Sally and Zara, our steady, reliable, loveable German Shepherd) at my parents' home. My mum had cooked a leg of pork and an apple pie for dinner, both of which were cooling on the side in the kitchen, out of harm's way. When we came home, the dogs had eaten the lot – well, they had left the bone. Fish and chips all round that evening – for the humans anyway.

Then there was the time when I decided to make an apple pie. Not being the best pastry cook, this was quite a brave decision for me. I made up 12 ounces of raw pastry, and, following Delia's instructions, prepared to wrap it in cling film to allow it 'to rest'. My poor ball of pastry didn't get the time to draw breath never mind rest! By the time I had rinsed my hands and torn off a piece of cling film, Sally had wolfed the lot. The thing is, I didn't see or hear her, and, being the sort of absentminded person I am, thought I must have moved the pastry elsewhere. I searched all work surfaces and the fridge until I looked at Sally and realised the truth about what had really happened.

Three months before I got married, I started to make sugar almond favours. I prepared all the ribbon and lace, and my mum ordered a kilo (about 500 sweets) of white, imported Italian sugared almonds.

Mum brought the sweets to the flat. Not long after she had left, I thought about moving the box of almonds to a safe place. Too late – when I picked it up, the lid was soggy and chewed, and only about five sugared almonds were inside, which Sally obviously hadn't had time to eat. As nature took its course over the following days, it became obvious that, in her rush, she had swallowed the lot whole.

When we lost Sally, we tried to convince ourselves that two dogs (Zara, a German Shepherd, and Wincey the mongrel) were enough. We kidded ourselves for about five months and then rescued another black-and-white Springer Spaniel – Purdy.

She has her own little character and really makes us laugh. The way she lies on her back and juggles a tennis ball between her front paws is just one of her little tricks. However, the day I would have sold my soul for a hidden camera in the kitchen was the day I made fresh pizza.

I prepared the dough and lined a baking tray (raw pizza dough is very elastic). I left the dough to prove, but when I returned to it, there was a very large 'tongue' of dough hanging over the side of the tray and down the cupboards.

Temptation had obviously got the better of Purdy and she had grabbed hold of a piece of dough, not expecting it to stretch and stretch the more she pulled. The look of puzzlement on her face must have been a picture; I imagine she admitted defeat and walked away, as there was only the one set of teeth marks on the dough, and she was nowhere in sight.

Unprovoked Attacks

Colin Plum, dog trainer and Guide Dogs volunteer

Toby, a tri-coloured Border Collie, was one of the brightest, quickest dogs I have ever worked with. All I had to do was hold on to the lead. He seemed to have an instinctive feel for what was going to happen next. So, over the years, I took up competitive dog training with him.

On my first competitive round, I had only gone about a couple of yards when the judge stopped me and asked, "What are you running for?"

"Well," I replied, "this is my first time with a Border Collie, as I have only had Labradors before."

The judge went into hysterics and said, "Well, I'll remember to bring my running shoes next time, and you had better bring yours too." Although I didn't get a prize, the judge very kindly gave me some tips afterwards.

On another occasion, the same judge was in another ring to the one I was in. That day, Toby was working well and so was I. Afterwards I thanked him for his tips. He said, "That dog and you will do well if you persevere." He was right.

Toby was remarkable. The number of rosettes that came our way were all down to him. I still have them adorning my office. He was special, and we were always in tune with each other.

One night, I took Toby on to the unfenced field that faced our house. It was quite a pleasant evening, until a dog, who was in the care of a very young girl, immediately lunged at Toby. They locked their jaws, and I could not part them. The dog was far too big for the girl, and I told her to hold the dog's lead, but not to get close to either dog.

I couldn't do much at that point, so I literally herded the dogs, still locked together, until I was opposite our house. I shouted to my elder son to give me a helping hand, and we grabbed a mouth each and took them apart. Fortunately, our fingers were still intact.

The young girl was somewhat concerned about getting back to her parents in one piece. So my son took Toby into the house and I went back to the youngster and her dog, took them home and explained the situation.

The parents were somewhat concerned, but were glad that no real damage had been done. But what stupidity to allow a child to be in charge of that size of dog! In another situation, she might well have been badly maimed.

Another time, my two dogs, a Labrador bitch and Toby, were paddling in a very shallow stream, in public woodland. I was waiting to call them back when, quite out of the blue, I was attacked by a very irate elderly couple. They were both only about four feet high and they were, at least, 70 years old.

The husband started to hit me and I was trying to get away without having to hit him back. My dogs were frantic when they saw what was happening to me, so I put them in the Down position. The wife kept hitting me with her umbrella and had the cheek to say that I had attacked her husband.

I had no choice but to defend myself, so I pushed the man away and told the wife that if she didn't take her husband away, I would put them both in the river. The dogs were still in the Down-stay, as I had told them. I was proud of them and they had a special treat that day. The couple, apparently, often prowled the area, shouting at people on some pretence of imaginary vandalism.

Traffic Sense

Jenny Moir, head of PR, Hearing Dogs for Deaf People

Dodger was a crossbreed. His recipient, Alison, was taking him for his usual walk and they came to a busy junction controlled by lights.

When the 'green man' came on, Alison started to cross, but Dodger dug his heels in, and refused to move. Alison stopped to see what was wrong with him, and the next moment a bicycle rushed round the corner and through the red light.

Dodger had heard the bike coming, when Alison had not. He'd used his initiative to stop her from stepping into the road, where she would undoubtedly have been involved in a collision with the bicycle.

End Game

Trevor Turner, vet and author

A lovely tempered Basset arrived at my clinic with a large anal abscess. I suggested admittance, incision and drainage. The owner declined. She did not want her dog "cut about".

I suggested that the abscess was of such a size that it was unlikely to respond to antibiotic treatment but was persuaded to try. Two tablets were prescribed three times a day.

A few hours later, I received a phone call from the owner explaining that she was having great difficulty getting the antibiotics in. Puzzled, since in my experience this bitch would eat anything, I asked her what she was doing.

"Trying to push them up her bum, of course," she said. "Two, three times a day."

The moral of this is, be specific in your labelling. "Give two tablets three times a day" is just not good enough. You must emphasise where the tablets should be given!

Brotherly Love

Dr Keith Barnett, Consultant Opthalmologist, Animal Health Trust

This is a true story that occurred many years ago, while I was a house surgeon at the Beaumont Hospital of the Royal Veterinary College.

The owner was an OAP with a small crossbred terrier bitch. His complaint was that his dog's abdomen was increasing in size; in all other respects, the dog was in normal health, with no diarrhoea, vomiting, or thirst, and with a good appetite.

Examination soon showed that the bitch was pregnant, and, on informing the owner, he said that this was impossible. On careful and prolonged questioning about the possibility of a mating, everything was denied, and, in desperation, I asked if he had another dog in the house. "Yes," he said, "but it is her brother!"

Matchmaking Magic

Jack Johnstone, Field Director, Dogs Trust (formerly National Canine Defence League)

Our rehomers are wonderful people who go that extra mile to give a dog another chance. Often, dogs are with us through no fault of their own. The death of an owner, marriage break-ups, or job losses can all be responsible, or perhaps the dog has strayed and cannot be reunited with his or her owner.

We rehome many thousands of dogs every year, and the vast majority have a story to tell about past and current lives.

Occasionally, a letter will come to us that hits a chord and brings home to me the joy and satisfaction of finding the right home for the right dog, and the right dog for the right home. Here's one:

Dear NCDL,
Ten years ago, we came to one of your rehoming centres, looking for a small dog to keep me company while I was away driving my lorry.

At the back of the kennel, lying in a box, was a thin, sad-looking Springer called Ben.

"What about the quiet Springer?" says I. In fact, Ben was anything but quiet. Despite his over-enthusiastic approach to life, he settled into the routine in the lorry very well. After a few days, he even learned to sit in my driver's seat if he wanted to watch me loading – he used the mirrors to do this!

Miles and miles of mountain-walking kept him lean and fit. In the winter, I had to bite the snow from between his paws every five miles or so, as it 'balled up'. He would trust me completely, and, on steep climbs down, would jump into my arms from the ledge above.

For every one of my miles, he did two. On Helvellyn in the Lake District one winter, we did the ridge in poor conditions. Stuck out on an exposed ridge, I got Ben inside my coat and dug into the snow until the wind subsided. Then we came off the ridge, both smiling. We did it!

Ben was a menace in the house, he never stole food, never bit anyone, didn't bark much, but boy did he pad pad pad – round and round. If he didn't get a good 10 miles a day, he was awful to live with. I took to taking him mountain-biking – he loved it, but, as he got older, I would often have to give him a little carry.

Never had a dog before. Until I had to take him to the vet's tonight, I suppose I never realised how much I loved the silly old bugger. I probably spent more time with him than with my wife. He got old, I nursed him for 18 months, but today he went.

Thank you for letting me share his life.

Graeme Lewis, Wales.

The Boxer Poodle

Andrew Edney, vet

Cruelty cases are always highly stressful for everyone concerned, but at least this one had a happy ending. The subject was a Miniature Poodle. He was known as Doodle the Poodle.

Doodle lived in a multi-dog household where he was bottom of the family hierarchy. Some youths (who were subsequently dealt with by the courts) had abused the animal and thrown him into a quarry, breaking both his front legs. All this was long before elaborate internal fixation techniques became commonplace. We put a substantial plastercast on each of the legs, so that

Doodle looked something like a toy soldier carrying two heavy rifles.

Our patient very soon became accustomed to these impediments and managed to walk quite well within a few days. Then, he learned that he could adjust his position in the pecking order by giving his bullying housemates a good clout with one, and then the other, plastered leg.

After about six weeks, he had clouted his way to become the master of the household canine population.

Then, the time came for the plasters to come off and you could see that Doodle was very disappointed about this. But he was too clever to be pushed back to his old place as the lowest member of the household.

After a few days, he learned that he did not actually have to hit the other dogs to maintain his supremacy. He only had to make threatening gestures as if he was still plastered. He never looked back.

Canned Laughter

Viv Alemi, vet

A greedy Labrador puppy got his head stuck in a can of food and it required a can opener and a lot of patience for the tin to be successfully removed.

Shooting Star

Mary Holmes, dog trainer and author

With more than 40 years of training dogs for film and television work, my late husband, John, and I obviously had a great many through our hands. All had their good points, but only a handful had 'star' quality.

One was Mandy, a Pekingese. We did not really want a

Peke – they are not noted for their trainability – but we urgently needed one for a film part. We heard of Mandy through a local breeder; Mandy had been returned to her at 10 months for being out of control. A Peke? Surely not. Mandy seemed healthy and friendly so we brought her home and realised almost at once that here we had something special. I think her only problem had been boredom and frustration.

In no time at all she, literally, took over. At that time, we had about 25 working dogs of all shapes and sizes, with about half a dozen living in the house, including Guidewell Ivan, the then pack leader. But from day one he let Mandy do exactly what she liked – from pinching his bed to sitting on top of him.

Mandy took to film work like a duck to water and was very easy to train and quick in the uptake. If anything, she preferred television work.

In those days, most shows were live with an audience. On rehearsal, Mandy would often give a lifeless performance, which worried any directors who had not worked with her before. But once the audience was in place, she revelled in the attention and applause, and really sparkled.

Mandy worked with many famous stars, such as Stanley Baxter, Ingrid Bergman, Terry Thomas and Peter Sellers, to name just a few.

In the first scene of her first film, *Kill or Cure*, she had to rush back and forth through an apparently solid door. We taught her to go through the cat flap at home. In the studio, she soon got the hang of the solid flap and worked enthusiastically. But on rehearsal, a props boy was heard to say, "Cor, did you see that dog? It went straight through that ruddy door!"

In *The Yellow Rolls Royce*, with Ingrid Bergman, there was a scene depicting a bombed-out square in Austria. Ingrid and Mandy were hiding under a broken table while firecrackers and loud explosions went off all around them, and a roof was blown off. They were

meant to be terrified. Ingrid, as you would expect, really looked the part.

Unfortunately, Mandy thought it great fun and kept looking out. So we had to re-shoot, with Ingrid holding Mandy and hiding her face.

In another film, Mandy was in a scene at St Ermines Hotel in London. She was supposed to be stranded on a narrow window ledge, five floors up, where she would be rescued by a fireman on an extending ladder. Mandy seemed okay, but John put a 400lb breaking line on her – just in case.

He then lay on the floor behind, holding the line. When he heard the fireman talking, it was his cue to release the line, which he did. When he saw the rushes, as the fireman arrived, Mandy wagged her tail and licked his face!

In another film, *Diamonds for Breakfast*, with Rita Tushingham and Warren Mitchell, Mandy had to pull a small troika filled with cardboard Easter eggs through the entrance hall at Blenheim Palace, on to the forecourt, where she was to stop before the flight of stone steps. We were a bit worried that, as I was right down at the bottom, she might not hear me telling her to stand and stay, so we put a line on the troika just in case.

Unfortunately, as she went off at a brisk trot, the line caught in a door and broke. The momentum carried Mandy forward and she careered down the steps, Easter eggs flying all over the place. Unhurt and unfazed, she promptly did another take and stopped exactly on her mark when told to do so.

Also in *Diamonds for Breakfast*, she had a scene where she was put in a large entrée dish, covered with the lid, and wheeled down to the dining room on a trolley. Again, we were worried that she might not like it, but after we had propped up the lid enough to give her some air, off she went. On being uncovered, she just sat looking around, no doubt hoping for applause.

Mandy appeared in innumerable television shows, being a particular favourite of Michael Mills (later to become head of light entertainment at the BBC) although he was convinced that he disliked Pekes.

We were working in the studios with a collie-type when Michael said he needed a small dog the following week on the *Stanley Baxter Show*.

It was to pop out of Stanley's jacket, like a rabbit with a magician. I said I had just the dog, a Peke. "No thanks," was the answer, "not a Peke. Nasty, snappy little beasts."

The next day, we were working up there again and I took Mandy along, keeping her out of sight. Standing behind Michael (who did not know I had her), I called his name, and, as he turned round, dropped Mandy in his arms where she went completely floppy (something she always did when carried). Needless to say she got the job.

One year, we took Mandy along to the Easter London Harness Parade as we were going with a pony. We put Mandy in her troika, with a rabbit as a passenger. We put her down as we came up to the judges, and, although I am not sure dogs were allowed, she got a certificate and the rabbit a carrot, and both had their photos in the papers.

Mandy lived to be 15½ and always had her own birthday party. We put her troika in the hall, where guests filled it with presents, and she pulled it into the room for them to be opened.

Although only 10lb, Mandy had more guts than many a GSD or Rottie, not to mention a huge enthusiasm for life. We really missed her, and so did the dogs, when she went. We never had another Peke, but were always grateful to her for the fun she gave us.

Cash For Trash

Murray Simmonds, Sergeant, Ministry of Defence (Police Dogs)

This tale relates to a German Shorthaired Pointer, who sits by me as I write this. He is getting on for 11 years old, as near as I can gauge, but looks half that. He has never had a day's illness, despite his disgusting habits, and came to me by way of my brother 10 years ago.

My brother, Marcus, was working for a somewhat dubious character, who had a large collection of birds of prey. Marcus rang me to say he had acquired this fantastic Pointer, called Cash, which he intended to train to work with his falcon.

Several months passed when Marcus rang again to say

that, due to professional differences, he was leaving his present employment, and, as he had no fixed abode, could I find a home for this wonderful dog? His description of the dog and his abilities, such as steadiness to game and total whistle control, made me think that I would be able to place him.

Arrangements were made to have Cash brought to my home, but this went slightly wrong. A colleague of Marcus's delivered the dog, but we were on holiday at the time, and my wife's parents were looking after the house.

Upon our return, I was greeted by my somewhat agitated parents-in-law. They advised me that a half-starved maniac, who had eaten the leg of the dining room table and fouled every carpet in the house, had been delivered by a shady-looking character, who disappeared as quickly as he had come.

Cash was every bit as bad as the description. He had no concept of his name, did not even break stride at the sound of a whistle, had the foulest habits, and he looked as if he had never had a square meal in his life.

A couple of days passed and I managed to home him with my then boss. This lasted five days before his return for unacceptable behaviour (I won't linger on this, as the farmer never did find out).

A further two weeks passed, during which time my wife threatened to leave me on several occasions if Cash stayed a day longer. I then managed to find another home for him – this time with one of our police dog handlers. This lasted three days before his return.

Realising I was on to a loser with this rehoming saga, I proceeded to train Cash, a process that I am still actively involved in 10 years later.

I did manage to contact my brother during the first traumatic month, and, once I had finished the death threats, he proceeded to assure me the dog was wonderful when he had him. Then my brother went off on one of his walkabouts, not to be seen for several months. When we did meet, five months had elapsed since the arrival of Cash, who by now had just learnt his name. It was Christmas – the season of goodwill to all men – so I decided not to kill my brother after all. Instead I listened once again to the tales of some superdog.

Now, my parents and parents-in-law live only four houses apart. As I was staying with the latter, and my brother with the former, the reuniting of 'super Pointer' with his owner had not yet taken place.

So, as my brother entered the house, a look of disbelief was apparent as he uttered the words I will never forget: "That's not my dog!"

Now, the moral of this story is to be careful of shady characters who deliver dogs in your absence. To this day, the whereabouts of the real Cash are unknown and where this one came from is as much a mystery.

Something Different 2

Viv Alemi, vet

Several hamsters have been brought in over the years having developed lumps near their tails. Concerned owners are always relieved to hear that the lumps are, in fact, normal testicles.

Milk Monitor

Helen McCain, head trainer, Dogs for the Disabled

When teaching Elton, a yellow Labrador, the routine of fetching the milk crate and bottles from the front door and bringing it back to me in the kitchen, I hadn't appreciated that, despite his usual quiet, laidback approach to life, he did have his limits.

He demonstrated his frustration at the exercise by tossing his head and sending the milk crate hurtling towards me in the kitchen!

It was at that point that I realised he did actually understand the exercise.

Bird Brain

Jenny Moir, head of PR, Hearing Dogs for Deaf People

I was working with Willum, a Chihuahua, and his recipient, Christine. It was a return visit to check all was going well.

Christine reported that she was thrilled with Willum and his work, but she did say that when he alerted her to a sound, he didn't wait for her to ask "What is it?" but went immediately to the sound, often leaving Christine behind to catch up with him.

This wasn't a huge problem and was easily sorted, so, after a chat and a coffee, we started doing some practice.

Willum came and alerted beautifully when I set the phone ringing. However, before Christine could ask the question, the budgie, which up until now had been silent in a cage by the window, started chattering, "What is it Willum? What is it? Good boy..."

Willum, being the clever little dog he is, duly led off to the telephone, and Christine, of course being deaf, had no idea this had been going on!

Wish You Were Here

Nigel Hemming, artist

As an artist specialising in narrative paintings of working dogs, I am often asked where I get my ideas. The truth is that ideas come from absolutely everywhere. The key is to keep an open mind and look for them wherever you go. Of course, having dogs myself is, perhaps, the single most important factor.

Of all the images that I have created over the last 25 years, one in particular is my personal favourite. It is a picture entitled *Wish You Were Here*, and shows an old black Labrador, his left paw raised and placed on a garden bench. It is autumn, fallen leaves carpet the unkempt lawn, and an old, disused potting shed forms the backdrop to the scene.

In essence, it is a picture of an old, faithful dog, who has lost his master and is pining for him.

I wrote a small piece to accompany the print. It explains how the dog's master was a keen gardener and would spend many hours nurturing and tending to its needs. Ben, the old dog, was his constant companion, and, on summer evenings, they would sit together – the old man on the bench and Ben by his side – appreciating the results of the old man's labours.

The old man having passed away, the garden has become neglected and forlorn. Old Ben is pictured mourning his passing by the bench upon which his master and he had spent so much time. It is an image that is full of pathos; indeed, many people have told me that they find it so sad that they could not live with it. So what drove me to paint such a heart-rending image?

The roots of the piece are two-fold. The first influence is a work by my favourite dog painter, Sir Edwin Landseer. It is an image entitled *The Old Shepherd's Chief Mourner*. The setting is a 19th century Scottish bothie. Centre stage is a draped coffin with mourning bows scattered over it. The bothie is obviously that of the coffin's occupant.

Many poignant and personal items are shown in the painting of the shepherd's former life. Most significantly, pressed against the coffin with paw raised, the old man's faithful dog sits motionless and pitiful, left to grieve alone by the mourners who have so recently departed from the scene.

It is my favourite narrative dog painting – bar none. However, whereas the Victorians were obsessed by death and welcomed such morbid scenes, we are less tolerant today of imagery that is so unambiguous, and a painting of a coffin would be – if you will excuse the pun – the 'kiss of death' to its commercial appeal. My tribute, therefore, had to attempt to encompass some of the emotion but without the specifics.

The second element that influenced my painting of *Wish You Were Here* was a true story conveyed to me by my wife, Sue.

In 1980, Sue's father, Les, was tragically killed in a car accident. Sue and I were not married at the time, indeed we were not even together, and, sad to say, I never met Les.

One night, some time after the accident, Sue and her mum were sitting in their living room. Old Mick, Sue's dog, was curled up in front of the fire. Les had never professed to have much time for Mick, referring to him as, "That perishing pooch". Nevertheless, Sue would say that when Les thought no one was looking, he would give Mick a surreptitious pat on the head.

As Sue and her mother sat and watched TV, Mick suddenly got up and walked across the room to where Les's chair stood. No one had been permitted to sit in the chair since the fateful day. Mick placed his chin on the seat of the chair, wagged his tail a couple of times, then turned and re-traced his steps to his former position in front of the fire.

It was several years later that Sue related the story to me, and, from the moment that I heard it, I knew that, one day, I would paint an image that celebrated this moving incident. In some ways, it is a tribute to a man whom I never knew, but to whom I owe so much.

Wish You Were Here may not be the best narrative dog painting that I have produced, but its merits as a piece of work are irrelevant. For me, it is certainly the most personal and significant.

Poaching Ideas

Ivan Haley, animal welfare specialist

In the late 1950s, I lived on the outskirts of a large

Yorkshire town. The Staffordshire Bull Terrier was, then, a none-too-well-known breed. I had an adult dog, Rocky, who was a friend to everyone, except other dogs. No matter what, he wanted to fight them all.

During my walks, I regularly saw a man in his late fifties riding a bike – not so unusual, except he had one leg shorter than the other. His cycle had a pedal with built-up wooden blocks, to allow him to ride. Even more unusual, he always wore a long, fawn mac. As a result, I always assumed he was a 'flasher'. He worried me a little as he seemed to study me. I always hurried by, as he made me feel so nervous.

One day, Rocky was in fine form, trying to get off the lead and destroy some other canine, when the guy, who was known locally as 'Limpy' (those days were not very politically correct), sidled up to me. It was a scorching hot day, but still he was wearing the long mac. He asked me about Rocky – what his breed was, etc. Then he asked if he would catch rabbits and rats. I said the breed would, but a rabbit was a fast-moving animal. He then said he wanted to show me something, and started to unbutton and open his mac. "My God," I thought, "he thinks I am that way."

On opening the coat, he showed me a long, deep pocket, which was fitted inside. He put his hand in and pulled out a ferret. Rocky lunged but, luckily for the ferret, could not reach it. He explained he was a poacher, which was illegal of course, but I felt more at ease then, and fascinated. We left each other, and, when we met subsequently, we always had a natter.

Later, he came to my home, gave me his address and requested I visit him. He said he had something else to show me, and maybe we could make some money. That clinched it. So I made the visit.

He lived in a small terraced house and invited me through the kitchen into his front room. When he opened the door, the smell hit my nose. It was terrible. Inside, there were cages running all around the walls, containing rabbits, chickens, ferrets, and, to my surprise, an adult fox, who was racing back and forth.

I was gobsmacked. He explained that the fox was a vixen, and, obviously, could kill rabbits and other small animals. But he said foxes did not have the loyalty of a dog. He then asked if I would consider "mating Rocky to the fox, so that we could sell the offspring! With the cunning of the fox, and the aggression of the Staffordshire, we would have the perfect poacher's dog!"

After I closed my mouth, I asked him if he had tried before to mate the fox. He said he had to a Bedlington Terrier, without success. I then explained, with great difficulty, that the difference in the animals' chromosomes would never allow live puppies to be born. With this, both of us saw the money-making venture was finished before it started.

The meeting did not prove unfruitful though, because I used to find a poached wild rabbit on my doorstep for some time afterwards. Very nice they were too!

Soap Star

Jenny Kennish, breeder (Kinghern Leonbergers)

It was a grey, damp day in February 1998, when I set out with my Leonberger bitch, Gypsy, to make our regular Pets As Therapy (PAT) visit to the elderly care ward at Basingstoke Hospital in Hampshire.

A Leonberger is a rare breed of dog, originating from Germany and introduced into England in the 1940s. There is a story in the dog show world about a soldier who had brought a Leonberger back to England after the war. It was said that this soldier paid for the dog with bars of soap. This extraordinary tale was substantiated by later reports that the first Leonberger was exhibited at Crufts in 1948, but no more was known.

With Gypsy proudly wearing her distinguishing PAT Dog coat, we entered the men's hospital ward. We were soon spotted by a patient and a visitor. The visitor looked up and asked me, "What sort of dog is that?" When I replied that Gypsy was a Leonberger, the gentleman turned to his companion and said, "My mate brought one of those back with him after the war. He paid for him with 20 bars of soap."

I could not hide my excitement and interest, and rather apprehensively I asked, "Is your friend still alive?"

"Yes," replied the man, "I saw him two weeks ago. His name is Dave Gower."

The gentleman was not able to give me the exact address of where Dave Gower lived, but he directed me to the nearby town of Alton and described the location of the house.

The next day, I took Gypsy and our male Leo, Biffy, to see if we could find Mr Gower. Several times I had to stop and ask passers-by if they knew Mr Gower, and, eventually, I chanced to ask the right person, a neighbour.

With nervous excitement, I knocked on the front door of a large Victorian house. A short, frail, elderly gentleman answered the door. I introduced myself as the Secretary of the Leonberger Club of Great Britain and asked if he was the soldier who had bought a Leonberger dog in Germany, paid for with 20 bars of soap. Without changing his expression, he replied, "It was 10 bars, not 20!"

Gypsy and I had found Gunner Gower, the legendary soldier!

I was invited in, and, while we drank tea, Mr Gower showed me all the press cuttings and photographs of his Leonberger, Wilson. I could not believe my eyes and ears as the story unfolded, and Dave Gower could not believe it when I told him I had another Leonberger in the car.

There were tears in his eyes as he cuddled first Gypsy and then Biffy. He hadn't seen Leonbergers for more than 40 years! He did not know that the breed is now established in this country, or that there is a registered breed club.

Gradually, over the weeks, more of the extraordinary story unfolded. David Gower and his brother, John, were driver and co-driver in the Tank Regiment. Their Sherman tank had been converted into a mobile action control centre for the Battalion Commander. The Gower brothers were also the Commander's staff car drivers, when they were not in action.

At the end of the war, the Battalion was being held in reserve, in readiness for possible future military activity. They had moved to Hochosterwitz, a village in the foothills of the Austrian mountains, and there they made a base, at the foot of the castle, and awaited further orders.

With a twinkle in his eye, David told me that the

soldiers were not allowed to mix with the civilians, but the young women tempted them into conversation! He and his brother fancied the same lady, until David's attention was drawn to a beautiful, large dog wandering about the farmyard.

Determined to buy the dog, David haggled with the farmer, who eventually agreed to sell the dog for the rare war-time commodity – bars of soap. All the officers and men contributed their allowance and later helped to feed the dog as well.

David refused to take early demob, and remained in Austria until he could make arrangements for the dog – Wilson – to be brought to England. The obligatory six months in quarantine had to be endured before David was able to take Wilson to his home in Alton.

Wilson appeared at Crufts Dog Show in 1948, as a 'not for competition' entry. He aroused a great deal of interest and publicity, and became something of a celebrity.

In 1950, Dave successfully imported a Leonberger bitch, Lassie. Nowadays, we take that sort of achievement for granted, but during the austerity that followed the war, it was a major achievement. In 1952, two puppies were born to Lassie and Wilson. Sadly, that is where the breeding line ceased, as Dave found it increasingly difficult to import another bitch.

Gypsy and I continued to see Dave regularly, and, in 1999, he was made an honorary member of the Leonberger Club of Great Britain.

As time passed, Dave became very ill and our visits were sometimes to Basingstoke or Alton Hospital. Every time he saw Gypsy, he seemed to regain his strength, and in May 2001, Gypsy proudly carried her Crufts first prize rosette and card to his bedside.

She was the first in the veteran bitch class and willingly posed with Dave for a newspaper photograph.

At last his dream had come true – he was holding a Crufts First Prize, awarded to his Leonberger friend, Gypsy.

Dave died a few weeks later, in the summer of 2001. His funeral was a truly amazing day for his family and friends.

The coffin was attended by four Leonbergers, at both the church service and at the graveside, and because the dogs behaved so well, they were invited to join the family gathering that followed. Dave would have revelled in the atmosphere of the day.

Everyone was relaxed, and several mourners remembered Wilson and Lassie as they cuddled and stroked our Leonbergers.

The presence of the dogs brought a different dimension to the day, and it all happened because Gypsy had found that soldier... Dave Gower.

Up, Up And Away

Helen McCain, head trainer, Dogs for the Disabled

Working with dogs always leaves room for many surprises, both humorous and otherwise. Very often, it will be the dogs who show us the error of our ways with our training or confusing cues. However, for those of us who continue to learn from our canine friends, there are always those special moments that one cannot forget.

When teaching yellow Labrador Lilly to work with her new owner in their local supermarket, Lilly was asked to "Up", to place her front paws on the counter at the checkout in preparation to pass a purse across to the cashier. Lilly decided to take "Up" literally and launched herself on to the counter conveyor full of groceries. The look of surprise on her face as she was gracefully conveyed towards the cashier was a sight to be seen!

Learning Curve

Leonard Pagliero OBE, vice-president of the Kennel Club

Many decades ago, when I was starting out on my judging career, I was invited to judge several breeds (including Shetland Sheepdogs) at an open show in south Wales. Keen and eager, I arrived even before the doors were opened.

I judged all day to the best of my ability, and it was a splendid learning experience. Everyone was kind and friendly, and I enjoyed myself.

As people were leaving the hall, a lovely Welshman

with a wide grin on his face came over to me, shook my hand and said in a broad accent: "You're a nice fellow and I like you, but you know damn all about Shelties!"

I hope I have learned a bit since then!

The Night Shift

Pete Storer, retired police sergeant

The finest GSD that I ever worked with during my 16-year career with police dogs was a handsome long-haired specimen called Jager, affectionately known as 'Jag'. But even he had the occasional 'off' day.

It was 3am on a cold, wintry night, and Jag and I were struggling to remain awake for a further two hours to finish another nightshift. It had been a quiet night, and we had not been called to many incidents. Jag loved to work, and indeed went on to become Midlands Police Dog Champion of the Year and National Training Champion, not to mention winning other National Civilian Working Trophies.

I remember the radio bursting into life, and Jag jumping up in the back of the van expectantly. "Alarm – Pailton Working Men's Club," was the cry. This was an establishment a good five miles away, but it was always a good call – ripe for a burglar.

I started the Ford Diesel van, under-powered at 1600cc with me and my sandwiches, plus a 105lb dog and equipment in the back. The vehicle reluctantly lumbered towards Pailton and we eventually rolled up outside the club.

Jag and I had been there many times before, and stealthily approached together on foot so as not to disturb the intruders. Around the back of the premises, we found an open broken window, and I shouted a warning for the burglars to come out peacefully otherwise Jag would be sent in to get them.

There was no reply, so Jag went in, leaping straight through the window without flinching. Within seconds, he was barking madly some distance inside the club. So then it was my turn – I had to climb inside after my dog and retrieve my prisoner...

Wrong! Halfway through pulling my nimble body into the premises (I was 16 stones), my trousers got caught up on the little prong that held the window open. I was left dangling upside down, with my full bodyweight bearing down on the prong. Meanwhile, Jag was still barking frantically, punctured by the occasional pause to listen for his partner.

Ten minutes went by, and I was still upside down, having made no progress in releasing myself. Still, Jag was barking, but a little more wearily now. Eventually, I was joined by my colleagues, who arrived to see my feet sticking up in the air from the outside of the club. The swearing was intense!

Surprise turned to laughter when my colleagues heaved me into the club through the window. I ran in to Jag, swiftly followed by my work-mates, expecting to claim my prize. In the light of my torch, there was Jag, standing and barking at a coat stand in the corner of the bar, which was complete with a long overcoat and a trilby hat.

It was a long time before I – or Jag – lived it down!

Off His Box

Maurice Hall, former Guide Dogs trainer

A very experienced guide dog owner set out to do some shopping, and needed to post some mail at the beginning of the route.

After constant requests, the guide dog refused to find the post box at its usual location. After five minutes, the dog made a very determined deviation from the well-used route, stopped abruptly and barked twice. He had found their usual post box, which had now been relocated to a safer position.

Good Samaritan

Mike Stockman, retired vet, and General
Committee Member at the Kennel Club

It was a Friday evening. George, a male Labrador guide dog, hadn't been issued to his blind handler very long. He was obviously totally unaccustomed to being in harness with a human at the other end of it, who was plainly the worse for wear as a result of attending an office party. This particular handler, by the name of Gregory Snell, was a normally harmless lad of some 25 summers, who worked in central London.

George and Greg had presumably left the office at around 10.30pm. Greg's mates had steered them relatively safely down the escalator at Leicester Square and helped the two of them on to a Piccadilly Line train. They had travelled as far as Finsbury Park, where they had accompanied the pair up the 71-step spiral staircase on to the overground, where I first made my acquaintance with the two 'Gs'.

Incidentally, I had come from an evening of celebration at a pleasant watering hole not more than half a mile from Clarges Street (home to the Kennel Club). In evening dress, with a pair of relatively thin-soled shoes on my feet, I was intending to catch a taxi from Potters Bar station to my home about four miles away.

Gregory swayed gently in the icy breezes that characterised the platform any night in mid-December, and eventually became horizontal.

Finally, the Potters Bar train arrived. The friends poured Gregory (and George) aboard. When we arrived at Potters Bar, I looked around and there, sure enough, were George and Greg at the far end of the platform. Whatever instructions Greg was trying to convey to George were transparently not clear, as they were standing stock-still, until, once more, Greg landed abruptly on his coccyx. By this time, I felt that I couldn't leave the paralysed pair to the mercies of a bleak midwinter on a barren Potters Bar platform at 11.30pm.

Fortunately, guide dogs are not trained to protect their charges from inquiring humans, and George did not resent my offer to help Greg to his feet. We passed slowly, like a human-canine three-legged race, along the platform, down the lengthy slope, into the underpass, round the corner, and under the bridge. We then had to cross the road to start on the mile walk up a gentle slope to where dear Greg lived with his (probably by now) anxious mother.

Getting this information out of the still befuddled Greg, whom I had never met before, had taken some time. What was taking more time was that George was finding some difficulty in comprehending how a newly qualified guide dog, still with the lead on his harness, should try to obey the non-existent commands coming from his 'master' whose right arm was clutching a total stranger.

We arrived at a compromise. Greg took the lead off the harness and transferred it to George's collar. He then gave me the lead so that George was now on my left side while Gregory was clinging on for dear life to my right side.

The effect on George was electric! He decided he was now at liberty to relieve the pressure in his over-full bladder. He fired off his first shot at a courting couple locked in embrace only yards up the road home, and anointed every tree along the avenue. He also realised that he hadn't emptied his intestines for yonks and proceeded to foul the hitherto pristine grass verges of star-lit downtown Potters Bar.

We reached Greg's humble abode. I rang the bell and the lights came on. Mother opened the door, and George shot inside while Greg subsided with a sigh on to the bottom step.

I left them to it. It had been the last train. The taxi firm would have battened down the hatches long since. I trudged wearily home. The glow of evening alcohol had evaporated. My shoes were thinner-soled than I had realised. The thought of the Saturday morning surgery looming only about seven hours ahead didn't make life seem better. To cap it all, I had forgotten my front door key. I rang the bell. Five Keeshonds joined in the chorus.

The ever-loving opened the door. Except she wasn't all that ever-loving...

Christmas Message

Dick Lane, award-winning vet and author

Unfortunately, dogs eat things other than food. As a veterinary surgeon in practice, one of the commonest questions that I found myself unable to answer adequately was: "Why does my dog eat grass?"

I would suggest the need for additional fibre in the diet; perhaps that the green grass had a juicy flavour akin to that of the Kiwi fruit for ourselves. I was sure that the dog did not know he needed extra vitamins in his diet, and, in fact, the dog can manufacture adequate supplies of Vitamin C.

I also denied that dogs eat grass to make themselves sick, although perhaps this behaviour had saved the lives of some carrion-feeding dogs in the dim and distant past.

There could have been a genetic trait that had benefited grass-eaters over those who never ate grass but died of food toxins before they were old enough to breed. Only the coarsest leaf grasses will induce vomiting and some dogs eat just soft, fresh grass, so this theory is not very convincing.

Foreign bodies, the vets call them. Not a description of illegal immigrants but the scientific term used for an article or solid substance that should not be situated within the animal's body.

As a schoolboy 5th-former, I often used to walk to the public library in my lunch hour, and, on the way, I never failed to glance in at the little window of Swansea's PDSA (People's Dispensary for Sick Animals) clinic. Here was displayed an assortment of objects reputedly recovered from canine and feline patients.

The majority were pebbles of all shapes and sizes, perhaps a few seashells, and more mysterious dark objects that could have been leather, wood or other organic substances. There were shiny glass marbles, perhaps a fishhook, as it was a seaside town, and darning needles – often with lengths of cotton still attached, recovered from old ladies' cats.

This was in the wartime days before plastics became common, so there were no meat wrappers and none of those horrendous things called 'linear foreign bodies' that literally saw their way through an animal's small intestine before death occurs from peritonitis.

My early days in practice were without the benefit of X-rays. I became adept at fingertip palpation of the dog's abdomen. A history of a dull dog, hardly eating but without any specific symptoms of an infectious disease, suggested the need of a thorough patient examination. It was particularly rewarding when a moveable foreign body could be found in the abdomen by touch alone.

Young puppies might have a baby's rubber dummy stuck in the small intestine. Made of soft rubber, flavoured with milk, the dummies were easily swallowed; after passing through the stomach, they would partially inflate with food material and become wedged in the duodenum. This caused diarrhoea, severe illness and even death if undiagnosed and untreated.

Walnuts at Christmas time were to be expected as foreign bodies; smaller, smooth nuts went straight through. A Deputy Chief Police Constable, fond of golf, lost one of his practice balls, and, six weeks later, his black Labrador was brought in to me with a history of occasional sickness and weight loss. A stained but still white golf ball was recovered after an operation, much to the owner's amazement. Having an almost smooth exterior, and being too large to pass through the pylorus into the small intestine where it would have caused frequent vomiting, the ball had lain in the stomach for many weeks, causing little obvious trouble.

Not in the same locality was another foreign body that I could remove with my fingertips. A distressed cat was brought into the surgery with a watery, but slightly bulging, eye. Grass seeds can get behind the eyeball and cause this sort of problem. Careful examination and manipulation of the eyelids led at once to a small pellet of gunshot popping out between the eyeball and lower lid. The cat had presumably been in a field when a shotgun, fired at a long distance away, had allowed one of the lead pellets, at low velocity, to work its way past the eye. The resilience of the eyeball had prevented total blindness, if the cornea had been penetrated.

The most bizarre foreign body was one I found in a Labrador guide dog. It was in March and the dog had been referred to me at the Leamington Spa centre. An intestinal foreign body was diagnosed, confirmed by X-rays. Gas distension of the intestine appears as a black sausage on a plain X-ray, and this was a quick way of recognising some obstruction to the passage of food through the intestine. We went ahead with an operation under general anaesthetic, as there was some urgency.

The operation was not straightforward: there were signs of the obstruction, but a local inflammation and a peculiar irregularity to the intestine wall suggested a longer standing problem and a perforation might soon occur. After some manoeuvring of the intestine, an incision was made in the wall of the gut and an instrument was inserted inside to coax out the foreign body. There was absolute stillness in the operating theatre as this object was slowly extracted, and you could sense the tension in the air as the assisting nurses watched closely.

At last, the whitish spiky object came out. At first unrecognisable, there was a burst of laughter and much merriment when a swab was used to clean the object. It read… MERRY CHRISTMAS. The object was a plastic cake decoration.

Subsequently we learnt that the dog had helped himself to the frilly cake wrapper to which some icing sugar – and the plastic decoration – was still attached.

I am glad to say the dog made an excellent recovery and was able to return to work. Perhaps my schoolboy lunch-hour trips had not been entirely a waste of time.

A MERRY CHRISTMAS AND PLEASE REMEMBER THAT EATING THIS CAKE WRAPPER IS LIABLE TO CAUSE GAS DISTENSION OF THE INTESTINE!

A Patch In Time

Robert Killick, canine author, columnist and legend!

Ch. Kadabra Proper Charlie, a Welsh Terrier, was the best dog I'd ever bred. When he was trimmed and ready to show, he was like a child's toy on wheels. Every day in the show season, I spent at least an hour plucking and shaping him – a lot of work. I got him ready for the big Birmingham Championship Show, hoping he'd win the elusive third Challenge Certificate (CC), which would make him a Champion.

Charlie slept in the kitchen with a young bitch with whom he got on splendidly, or so I thought. Two nights before the show, I woke to the sound of a crazed snarling and hysterical barking.

I rushed downstairs and found the two of them locked in combat! Parting them, I found the bitch had a couple of superficial scratches, but she had managed to pull out a 4cm square patch of black hair from Charlie's side. Calamity! Charlie's skin was a pale grey, and, against the black of his coat, it looked white and really obvious. If the judge noticed it, Charlie would never win that third CC.

In the morning, I found a piece of greyish fabric, and glued scores of individual hairs on to it, making sure the hairs fell in the right direction. I cut it to the right size and trimmed the hairs to match.

It took hours. The next day, I went to the show with my kennelmaid, we put the grooming table as far as possible from human gaze, and, with my assistant masking my activities, I stuck the patch on using actor's wig glue.

It was a very good effort, and nobody could possibly have noticed. Thankfully, we won the class and Charlie's third Challenge Certificate. Great, he was a Champion! We had a few minutes to wait for the challenge for Best of Breed. Just as the judge was approaching, I looked down, and, to my horror, I saw the patch was hanging off.

I hastily tried to press it on, and only just succeeded, but Charlie didn't like being prodded about in the ring. He jumped about, spinning on his lead like a top, which he thought was very funny. I didn't stop him in case the judge saw the patch.

I didn't think it funny and neither did the judge – Charlie blew his chance and we lost. I didn't care, I still took home the best dog in the show and he was a Champion.

Doggie In The Well

John Uncle, London Canine Training Establishment

I was at Harlexton Manor to attend a week-long training course organised by Roy Hunter, with Gail Fisher and Wendy Volhard as the main lecturers. Driving through the gateway and on to the grand driveway, I was amazed to see in front of me a beautiful lake, with a bridge that I had to cross to reach the manor. I stopped the car on the bridge and allowed my two dogs freedom.

Below me, the swans, moorhens, and many species of duck swam gracefully. At this moment, my mind was concentrating on the peace and tranquillity that surrounded me.

I called my two dogs and continued my journey to the manor. The rest of the evening was taken up with dog-exercising, feeding, attending the welcoming lecture, a few drinks, and bed.

The next morning, I was up early. The sun was low and there was not a cloud in the sky. It was to remain like this for the rest of my stay. I set off at a good pace, my GSD, Ziggy, and Sally, a Springer, both ahead of me.

Once in the country, Sally flashed a rabbit from the undergrowth and started to pursue it. Ziggy took up the chase behind Sally. It was from this one encounter that Ziggy always followed Sally.

Sally had come into our lives through my daughter, who had obtained her from the RSPCA approximately six months earlier. She was about 18 months old, had a fear of all living creatures, and would lay down and quiver at the slightest sound. The list of her phobias would fill a book. I was sure that we could cure or control many of the behaviours that she displayed, given time.

Every few minutes, the dogs would return to me just to make sure I was following. Our walk had taken us near a small wood where both the dogs had disappeared into the undergrowth. As I could not see any pathway, I kept to the outside of the wood. Sally broke cover and started to run towards me; once she reached me, she sat by me and waited for Ziggy, who was normally only a few seconds behind – but not this time.

We both moved towards the position where Sally had broken cover. I called Ziggy, waited a few moments, and called again. Ziggy had never failed to respond to my call, and I started to worry. Sally looked up at me as if seeking permission to find Ziggy.

I decided to enter the wood with Sally and search for Ziggy. The going was hard; no one had been in this wood for a very long time. The brambles made it difficult; every thorn seemed to scratch at my arms and face. I could hear Sally in the undergrowth, searching for Ziggy or searching for more rabbits! I was becoming increasingly worried. Again I called; again no response.

A plan of action was needed; it was pointless just walking around in circles. I was sure that both dogs had been hunting rabbits.

What I needed to know was if Ziggy was still in the wood. Making my way to the top of the wood, I peered into the field, where there must have been 15 to 20 rabbits eating the young shoots. Ziggy had not come this way. I started to move to the other side of the wood – again more rabbits having their breakfast.

Moving towards the other side of the wood, Sally, who had been beside me, started to run towards the centre. I was determined to keep up with her. The distance we had covered was no more than 15 yards, when I found myself in a clearing approximately 10 yards square.

Very low to the ground, there was some form of plant life that covered the area. Sally was in the middle of the opening, looking down and then up at me. I knew my search was over.

Peering down into a well, I saw Ziggy standing there, looking up at me. He didn't appear injured. I could hear myself saying, "What are you doing down there?"

The well was actually an inspection chamber, measuring three foot squared and 14 foot deep. Down one side, I noticed four metal steps, which I descended. Bending down to see if I could lift him was impossible due to the lack of space. A decision had to be made. Ziggy had to be left while I returned to the manor for help.

My journey back took about a quarter of an hour. Within minutes, a rescue party was ready to return, equipped with a tow-rope.

Once back at the scene, it took minutes to free Ziggy by hoisting him up with the end of the rope. Two hours had passed from the time Ziggy had disappeared.

Ziggy died at the age of 13 and he never left my side for the remainder of his life. Sally also has gone. I believe that she and Ziggy are still trying to catch their first rabbit in the world of departed dogs.

In Dog We Trust

Keith Warwick, dog handler, Search and Rescue Dog Association

It was the Saturday before Christmas. I was at home with my feet up by the fire, but the telephone brought me to my senses. It was my Mountain Rescue Team Leader. "Can you turn out with your dog at first light tomorrow?" This was my first ever call-out with my newly qualified search dog. "Sure I can," I said. He gave me the details of the search and hung up.

The missing person was an elderly man with

dementia, who had gone missing from his residential home not far from where I lived. I took a brief look outside at the weather; the snow was horizontal, whipped up by gale-force winds. My mind started to race. I had trained with my dog, Graf, a German Shepherd, for more than two years to find missing people. Almost all of my searches had been in a mountain environment. Suddenly I was expected to look for someone at sea level, just minutes from home!

I didn't sleep that night. By 6.30am I had eaten my breakfast, and had packed my rucksack with food, a flask and the all-important radio.

I had to report to a small local police station, and was met by a red-faced police sergeant, who offered me a hot drink. I accepted this offer mainly because I didn't feel it would be right to refuse his hospitality. He told me that searches had been carried out within the immediate vicinity without success. Now the search was to be expanded. Other members of my local Mountain Rescue Team would be arriving to carry out a foot search.

As a dog handler working on my own, I was given a police radio in order that I could keep in contact with control. The radios that we used at that time were, at best, poor. As I remember, they needed ten 'pencil' batteries. Even then, their range was very limited. I recalled the last training session in North Yorkshire where I had been entertained by Terry Wogan for much of the day on my radio, but had been unable to make or receive calls. I reported the problem and was told, "Oh yes, they do that sometimes."

I stepped outside the police station into the half-light of a new day. If anything, the weather was worse than the night before. I couldn't help thinking of the poor man I was looking for.

I headed for the first part of my search – an empty factory. I was very anxious. Thinking back, I have no idea why I was so nervous; thankfully, Graf didn't seem to be fazed by my anxiety or by the weather – he was as keen as ever to begin his work.

Once we had cleared the factory, we moved on to the surrounding fields. We moved in a north-westerly direction, straight into the wind and snow, which stung my eyes and face. The fields were used as grazing for horses and ponies, but most were snug and warm in their stables. Those that were outside took what shelter they could from hedges and walls.

Suddenly Graf came running towards me, barking furiously. This signal indicates he has found something. However, I am ashamed to say that I didn't believe him! We were within half a mile of the residential home from where the gentleman had gone missing. It couldn't be him, could it?

Graf came in for a second time, excitedly barking and wagging his tail. I tried to look in the direction that he had come from but could not see what was causing him to get so excited. I then assumed that, as we were searching very close to houses, that he had picked up the scent of someone, perhaps in a garden. I told him to "Go find", but he looked at me as if to say, "That's exactly what I'm doing, and you're not interested."

Thankfully, Graf was a very tenacious dog and he insisted that he had found something and that I should go with him (exactly as he had been trained to do). I followed him, but still did not believe him – after all, nobody ever finds a person on their first search.

Graf took me to what at first appeared to be a bag lying over a fence. He barked furiously at it and returned to me. When I arrived, I was totally shocked. There was the face of the missing man. His eyes were open, but he was obviously dead. He appeared to have been trying to climb over the barbed wire fence and had become entangled. I can still see his tartan slippers, even after so many years.

My mind was racing. What should I do next? Report the find to my Mountain Rescue Team via a dodgy radio, or to the police on their set? I knew that it was important not to disturb the scene, but what should I do? Once again, Graf came to my rescue, presenting me with a stick to throw for him. The first thing a handler should do when their dog has a successful find is to praise their dog and reward him for doing such a good job!

I learned so very much from Graf during his time with me, but on that day I perhaps learned the single most important lesson – always trust your dog. He had remembered his training and did what he was supposed to do. I, on the other hand, had gone to pieces.

Every dog handler in every discipline of dog work remembers his or her dogs, past and present. I have had many dogs through my hands. Some have been better than others, but there will always be a place for my dear Graf. We went through so much together for the first time. He was a true friend and ally, who always kept me on the straight and narrow.

When he died at the age of 13, I was devastated. It took many months for me to get over his death. I will never forget him.

Hoagan's Howl

Audrey Plum, volunteer at Guide Dogs and Dogs for the Disabled

Hoagan was one of the first Dogs for the Disabled – the tenth, to be precise. He was a great help to his owner, who was completely wheelchair– or bed-bound. Hoagan would constantly have to pick up things and jump on to her lap or bed to give them to her, so he wasn't a very big dog.

The owner was often in hospital, and, during those times, we looked after Hoagan. One such visit lasted 14 months, so he was really one of our family and we knew him well. Unfortunately, his owner died in 1996, and so, obviously, he came to stay with us permanently.

We were able to take Hoagan to his owner's funeral at the Salvation Army Chapel in Stratford-upon-Avon, and he was very good and quiet, sleeping at our feet while the service was on. We all then moved to the crematorium a short distance away. There, he was just as quiet and slept at our feet, until the curtains began to move in front of the coffin when the body was starting its journey to be cremated. At this point, Hoagan stood up and let out the most awful noise. He just howled and howled until the curtains closed completely and then he stopped and was back to his normal, quiet, church-like demeanour.

What possessed him to howl like that, at that particular time? It unnerved us all to hear him. He had never howled in the years we had been looking after him, and he has never, ever howled since. Could he really have known what was happening?

He is now at least 17, maybe more (though he behaves more like an 11– or 12-year-old). We don't know his exact age because he was found wandering the streets of Coventry before being taken in by Frances Hay, the founder of Dogs for the Disabled, who then trained him.

Keeping Up With The Joneses

Sue Cottrell, dog trainer

A few years ago, some friends of mine, the Wilsons, moved into a new house. The road was quite exclusive – the houses becoming more and more up-market the further along it you travelled. The Wilsons' house was one of the first, and they would joke that they lived at the cheap end of the street.

Being sociable and outgoing people, it was not long

before my friends had become acquainted with all the families along the road. All, that is, except an elderly couple – the Joneses – who lived about two-thirds of the way along.

The Wilsons couldn't decide whether the Joneses were just intent on keeping themselves to themselves, or, as it appeared, thought themselves better than those around them. Whenever a neighbour would drive past the Wilsons' house, and they were on the drive or in the front garden, all would wave to each other in a friendly manner. Their relationship with some of the neighbours had even reached the point of reciprocal dinner parties.

Not the Joneses, of course! Whenever they drove past in their expensive and eternally spotless German saloon, their eyes were always fixed to the fore so that any friendly gestures from the Wilsons were either ignored or simply overlooked.

Now, it so happened that the Wilsons owned a little dog – a West Highland White Terrier, to be precise. It was generally agreed by all who knew the dog that he was one of the most attractive and adorable little chaps that you could possibly imagine. I must confess that I have never been one for small dogs myself; however, even I had to admit that Connor, as he was called, was really cute.

Mr Wilson would sometimes walk Connor along their road if he had not had a chance to take him to the nearby park for a longer run.

As their first summer in the new house approached, Mr Wilson was fascinated to observe that Mrs Jones was a keen gardener. This, in itself, was not surprising, as all the residents of the road maintained their gardens to the highest degree. It must be said, however, that the further along you went, the higher was the probability that a gardener was employed for this purpose. The Jones' bungalow was among these houses, and yet this was not the reason that Mr Wilson was surprised by Mrs Jones. What fascinated my friend was Mrs Jones' appearance.

On the occasions that Mr Wilson observed Mrs Jones working in the garden, she looked as though she was ready to receive royalty and serve them afternoon tea. Twin-set and pearls were the norm, her hair always coiffured immaculately, but perhaps the most surprising thing of all were the spotless white slacks and strappy, heeled shoes. Her only concession to practicality was the pair of bright yellow Marigolds that protected her well-manicured hands.

Gardening can hardly be described as a clean pursuit, and, quite rightly, most people who indulge tend to wear either old clothes or some kind of protective overalls. Nevertheless, Mrs Jones' appearance was always immaculate. She never appeared to acquire a single mark on her pristine trousers.

It is against this backdrop that the events of one Sunday that summer seem so surprising.

The Wilsons were working in their front garden that afternoon, attempting to compete with the mainly professionally cultivated frontages along their road. It was hot, and Mr Wilson, to whom gardening did not come naturally, was not enjoying cutting the lawn. Mrs Wilson, on the other hand, derived much pleasure from a touch of weeding and the tickling up of borders. Connor, the dog, was sprawled out on the newly mown grass, catching the summer rays.

The Wilsons looked up simultaneously as they heard a car approaching, ready with a friendly wave and a smile for whichever neighbour was about to pass. When they saw that it was the Joneses, they both hesitated, unsure whether or not to waste a greeting. To their great surprise (and perhaps a degree of discomfort), the large green car, spotless as ever, slowed down and stopped in front of the Wilsons' house.

For a brief moment that seemed to last forever, Mr Wilson mentally recapped the events of the last week or two, attempting to recall some incident that may have occurred to give rise to a complaint from the Joneses.

As the car halted, there was a perfunctory nod from Mr Jones in the driving seat while the passenger door opened and out stepped the well-groomed figure of Mrs Jones, resplendent in her brilliant white trousers and cashmere jacket.

The Wilsons, stunned by this unforeseen event, stood a little shell-shocked. Connor, on the other hand, was always ready to welcome anyone who cared to visit his patch. He rose from his recumbent pose and trotted across the lawn towards Mrs Jones. He had a veritable spring in his step, his tail was wagging happily and his long, thin tongue lolling from the heat.

In unison, the Wilsons called to Connor frantically, attempting to prevent the greeting that they knew from experience would follow his rendezvous with Mrs Jones' legs. Connor was oblivious to all of the Wilsons' commands; his compulsion to greet all new arrivals far outweighed his duty of obedience. The Wilsons inwardly cringed as the little white dog (who looked positively grubby against Mrs Jones' pristine slacks) jumped up to greet his visitor. The Wilsons held their collective breath as they awaited the anticipated outburst from Mrs Jones – but it didn't come. They gradually exhaled as, to their complete surprise, Mrs Jones bent down to fuss Connor – and I mean really fuss him!

After a moment that felt like an eternity, Mrs Jones looked up in the Wilsons' direction and proclaimed in a surprisingly broad Birmingham accent, "I only wanted to see your dog. I didn't want to talk to you."

The abruptness of the statement was tempered by the warm smile on Mrs Jones' face and it was apparent that she was being facetious. They chatted and Mr Jones came round to fuss Connor. It transpired that they had once had a Westie but had lost her some years ago. The Joneses proved to be pleasant, and a more friendly relationship developed from then on.

There is one last thing you should be told. As Mrs Jones re-entered the car after that first meeting, the

Wilsons noticed that the backs of her immaculate white trousers were streaked with Westie-sized, dusty pawprints.

Police Partner

Roy Hunter, retired inspector at the Metropolitan Police and handler of Abelard, the first Rottweiler born in England, and the first Rottie to be used by any police force

We had a call to a man who was disturbed when breaking into a farmhouse. Abby the Rottie appeared to have picked up a scent; he put his nose down and started tracking. I put a harness and line on him, and, keeping the line slack, started to follow. Suddenly, he leapt forward and went around a corner. He came back immediately with a duck in his mouth. I took the duck from him, and the duck, not knowing how close he'd come to being eaten, waddled happily away.

One late afternoon, Abby, searching for a suspect, had to get over a chain-link fence (which is quite difficult to navigate). With the help of a colleague, we got him over the fence and on to a garden shed a couple of feet away. Unfortunately, the shed was not very stable, and collapsed under Abby's weight. The irate owner stuck his head out of the house and threatened to sue the police. I told him it would not look good for the innocent dog, and he relented and we all had a laugh.

I was patrolling with Abby when four yobs approached. There was a clink as one of them dropped a knife. A man overtaking them whispered to me out of the corner of his mouth, "The ginger one!" I lined them up against the wall, with them facing me, and walked along the front telling Abby to sniff each one. I said to Abby at the first three, "Was it him?" When I came to the fourth, the ginger one, I said, "This one?" with slightly more inflection in my voice. Abby barked, and the yob said, "Okay it was me, I might as well admit it, I know your dog can prove it!"

I was half-way through my dinner at home when an area car came for me. They took me to a gravel pit full of water a few miles away, explaining as we went. A member of the public reported that a truck had been parked for some time about 20 yards from the water with a pile of clothes by the door. It was a beautiful, sunny day with picnickers all over the place.

The local nick wanted me to confirm that the driver was in the lake before they would call Thames Police out to drag for him. What chance did my dog have of knowing that? I went through the motions, bullshitting! Putting the tracking line on, I gave the command, "Zoo". Having been called out so suddenly, I hadn't had a chance to follow my usual routine of giving Abby a drink first. We'd had a long, hot journey in the car and he was thirsty. As I'd anticipated, Abby pulled me straight from the driver's clothes to the water. "He's in there," I said confidently.

Thames Police were also confident; they dragged the water and pulled a body to the surface whereupon it slipped off their line back into the murky depths. "Never mind," said the sergeant. "It'll come up again in about 48 hours." The cynical cops then ran a book in half-hour periods, and one of them won around £30 – quite an amount in those days.

Abby, unlike many dogs, was not in the habit of barking when in his compound. However, he did twice. On the first occasion, one morning, it was discovered that a car outside next-door-but-one had been stolen. On the other occasion, a house that diagonally backed on to us had been burgled.

One evening, I was with Abby in the back of Yankee 4 – Tottenham's area car – when we passed a fracas on the pathway outside a shop. As I didn't want the paperwork involved with someone being bitten, I left Abby in the car and went with the other officers to quell the fight. Unfortunately, we had left the car window open. Suddenly, I heard a scream and a clang of something metal hitting the pavement. On turning, I saw Abby holding on to a man's bum. On getting him into the nick, the man's only comment was, "I wouldn't mind, but it was the indignity of it all!"

Hospital Visit

Kay White, author and journalist

Our white Boxer bitch, Pola, had been staying in the new Small Animal Centre at the Animal Health Trust at Newmarket for two weeks while attempts were made to sort out a skin problem, possibly connected to a food allergy.

Pola was very unhappy, although the nurses tried hard to cheer her up, taking her up to their staffroom at break times so she had a change of scenery and letting her make new friends.

In the hospital, there is a very long corridor, all new and shining, which leads from the kennel ward through the reception area and ultimately upstairs. When, after a miserable fortnight, we went to fetch Pola, a favourite nurse brought her from the kennel and together they started the long trek up the corridor. Pola walked slowly, with her head down, and looked as if she had given up on happiness.

We waited, with our senior Boxer on a lead at the end of the corridor because we were diffident about going into a sterile area. We were shocked that Pola was demonstrating such misery. But then, as she drew nearer, Pola obviously saw a Boxer in the reception area. She became a little more alert; and then she recognised that tall brindle outline... she realised the Boxer was her friend, Holly, from home.

Pola continued to show some pleasure but not very much – until she arrived at the foot of the stairs where we were waiting. Then, as she approached the stairs to go drearily up to the nurses' restroom, she saw us and melted into sheer joy.

I was impressed that it was obvious that seeing another Boxer was Pola's first key to recognising her owners. Can it be that people look very much alike to dogs, but canine companions are distinctive?

I will never forget the deep sadness and depression that had enveloped Pola since we left her, even though she had been in the very best, most sympathetic care. But her stay was worthwhile – she was found to be allergic to all foods except white fish and rice, and on this diet she lived to be an old lady of 13 years.

When she died, peacefully at my feet one evening, her vet sent her flowers, with a card addressed to "a very brave little dog". How can we ever deceive ourselves into believing that dogs are disposable objects?

Bridge Too Far

Maurice Hall, former Guide Dogs trainer

My father was walking his Golden Retriever, Digger, on their regular route around the golf course. They came to the old, wooden footbridge over the rail track, but the dog refused to use the bridge either on, or off, the leash. Subsequently, they had to return home via another route. It was late spring and there were very strong winds. That same night, the bridge collapsed on to the rail track.

Sage And Sagacious

Murray Simmonds, Sergeant, Ministry of Defence (Police Dogs)

Jessica was an English Springer Spaniel, bred by a good friend of mine who lived in Suffolk. Incidentally, she was born in the bomb dump at RAF Bentwaters, but that is another story.

Falconry is my all-consuming passion, and Jessica turned out to be an excellent finder and flusher of game, working in harmony with my goshawk, a Finnish male called Sage.

Now, a falconer's dog must be completely steady towards the hawk. They must never touch or interfere with them, and this golden rule is taught to them from the earliest age. An angry goshawk on his quarry will often remind the dog of this with a swift flash of his talons. Jessica was a quick learner, and, being a very sensitive dog, she always kept her distance.

In the autumn of 1988, I was hunting waterfowl on the River Avon in Wiltshire, supervised by two river keepers. Jessica was working the reeds, and a coot was flushed. Sage gave chase and took the coot in the middle of the pool. A fit goshawk will not give up its quarry lightly, and Sage showed no intention of releasing his prize. The coot proceeded to dive, dragging Sage under.

Now, being a bloody awful swimmer, and with no assistance coming from my two colleagues, I started pulling off my attire with the intention of diving into this deep pool to rescue Sage before the coot drowned him. Without warning or command, Jessica took to the water and swam towards my fast-submerging goshawk. Realising she might save the day, I urged her on. Upon reaching Sage, Jessica took his tail feathers in her mouth, turned for the bank, and swam towards me. I reached down and took Sage off her (the coot was still firmly in his feet). He was soaked and close to drowning.

My delight at recovering the goshawk, and not having to drown myself, was made all the more special by Jessica's actions. All her life, this little dog had been taught never to touch a hawk, under any circumstances. But she had realised by my panic and distress that she could help. Experiences such as this have made me realise that some dogs are capable of conscious thought.

Pulling Power

Colin Plum, dog trainer and Guide Dogs volunteer

Most dog clubs have presidents or other dignitaries. We have an excellent president in the person of Geoff Love, a well-known bandleader.

Geoff and his wife, Joy, had two Great Danes. Both

Geoff and Joy were very busy, but always ready to honour their commitment to the club.

On one occasion, Joy brought a new Dane puppy to the club, which she wanted to interact with other dogs and people. I suggested that, for the first 'trial run', Joy would have a lead on one side (the side she usually worked on) while I took the other side. So off we went.

The Dane was more like a bucking bronco than a pup – he was twice the size of the average GSD. Eventually, we had some success and sat down for a breather. However, the pup decided to do the same, but half of him was sitting on my lap and the other on Joy's, who said, "He likes you or else he would ignore you!"

I had no more comment because I had no more breath left, much to the amusement of the club members. He got big very fast, but settled down, and was a 'wow' with the public when he went into the ring.

Some time later, Joy took him on lead to the park; he saw another dog and took off dragging Joy as well. She had the lead end over her wrist and could not release it, so he pulled her for about 20 yards or so until two park-keepers caught him.

The last time I saw him, he had calmed down and had got a few rosettes as well.

Experimental Breeding

Stephen Wright, former Guide Dogs trainer

My story is set in the early 1970s at the Forfar Guide Dogs centre, where I was the training manager.

I also had a few dogs of my own, which included an Airedale Terrier stud dog. One evening, while I was away on business, my wife had just put the boys in the bath when the front-door bell rang. Outside was a notorious local poacher, who had the reputation of being "the meanest man in Angus" – a well-contested title, which should command the respect of any skinflint. At his side was his Lurcher bitch, a cross between a Greyhound and a Deerhound, elegant in her blue, wiry coat.

"Can I mate my bitch with yon hairy dog of yourn?" he inquired.

"If you can just wait until I've got the kids out of the bath," my wife replied. Unfortunately, the dog had, by this time, become aware of the bitch's presence, and had not only arrived on the scene but was already in the process of consummating the relationship! Leaving the happy couple coupled, with the Lurcher's owner leaning against the front door with a fag in his mouth, my wife returned to the children. By the time she came downstairs again, the man and his dog had disappeared into the night.

Now, in my book, you either get a stud fee or a pup. Our night visitor had offered neither, and, because of his reputation, we felt exploited and rather aggrieved. Accordingly, when we had calculated that the litter would be about six weeks old, we set off to make a surprise call. Not purely by chance, we arrived when he was at work. However, his wife – a charming and gullible soul (she must have been to marry him) – was more than happy to show us the pups.

Expressing surprise at her husband's absence, I said, "We've come over to pick our puppy. We didn't know he wouldn't be here."

"That's okay, I'll tell him you've been. I'm sure he won't mind." It was the work of a moment to lift the pick of the litter, bid goodbye to our hostess, then drive off in a cloud of guilt and dust.

"Now what do we do with it?" my wife demanded. "He's not going to be happy with us. We'd better hide it somewhere and tell him we've already sold it."

At the time, as well as the official puppy-walking scheme, there was an informal, voluntary one being run by a charming and enthusiastic man called Hugh Harris.

Somehow I managed to convince the centre manager that a Lurcher puppy was probably the guide dog of the future, and that he could be the pioneer of this new breed of guide dog. I argued that here was a dog that had been bred to use its eyes, that had lived in a one-to-one relationship with its owner for thousands of years, that had no physical, hereditary defects and was long-lived. I explained that the Lurcher thinks ahead and would give a smoother 'ride' to its blind owner, compared to the Labrador, which thinks no further than the end of its nose. I was also able to quote that I had previously trained a Lurcher as a guide dog and that, by some quirk of fate, the sire of this particular puppy was himself the full brother to the only Airedale Terrier guide dog. It was an opportunity that could not be missed.

The upshot of all this was that, rather than commit the puppy to the formal puppy-walking scheme, we would tuck it away on Hugh's unauthorised scheme. Hugh himself, with his boundless enthusiasm, was more than ready for the challenge and volunteered to walk this special prototype puppy himself. Unfortunately, he lived in the middle of the rural Gleneagles estate. I had visions of the puppy chasing rabbits, hares, grouse, sheep, and anything else that moved. I earnestly exhorted him to keep the dog away from livestock of any kind.

The months went by, and the puppy turned into a charming and well-behaved animal. Each day, Hugh would leave his Perthshire retreat and motor into Glasgow, to exercise the dog in the temptation-free city parks. All the time, the dog remained blissfully ignorant of the joys of the chase.

In the fullness of time, she returned for training. It was an effortless education and she progressed speedily, patrolling the streets of Forfar and Dundee with ease.

A replacement dog was needed urgently for a young man who earned his living as a musician. His lifestyle was one of trains, tubes and clubs. "Ah, good, we thought – no chance for the dog to get into bad chasing habits."

In addition, Mr X requested a dog that did not look like a guide dog, as he wanted to avoid any kind of 'sympathy vote' in his work. We told him we had a suitable dog, but that it was a Lurcher. "Great!" he replied. "I used to have one of those when I was a boy."

The pair rapidly formed an efficient team, but we should have known it was too good to last. One day, travelling through Forfar on a training route, the dog departed from her planned route and turned towards the kerb edge, where she sat facing out into the traffic. Her master heard sounds of workmen on the pavement. Deducing that the path was obstructed, he decided that he would need to go out into the road to circumnavigate the obstacle. As soon as there was no traffic, he urged the dog forward, encouraging her to make a speedy return to the sanctuary of the pavement.

To his satisfaction, he felt the dog step up after only a few yards, and lifted his own foot to meet the rising kerb. Unexpectedly, he felt not stone under his shoe but springy wood. He was walking up a ramp. His senses told him that he was in an enclosed space, and one that had a peculiar smell. Feeling about him, he discovered the truth – the dog had left a perfectly clear pavement to walk him into a furriers' van, where she sat, breathing in the heady scents.

On his return home, he submitted regular working reports. His first week read something like this:

"Have travelled some 600 miles this week, including trains and planes. The dog has been excellent and behaves brilliantly in the clubs. Oh, and I've been up two trees after squirrels and across a field after a rabbit!"

On questioning him, it transpired that he had forgotten to tell us of his impending move from his city flat to rural Surrey. Neither had he bothered to mention that, to get anywhere, he had to walk a mile-and-a-half down a country lane to the local station. Once he understood why the dog suddenly lunged forward, he got used to dropping the harness handle and holding the lead until the moment had passed, upon which the dog would readily resume her role as a guide.

The years passed and I lost track of the two of them.

Then, unexpectedly, on a visit to another centre, I was told that Mr X wanted to see me in his room, where he was training with a new dog.

"I'm glad you've come," he said, "because I know how involved you were with the old dog."

"What happened to her? I thought she would go on for years."

"That's what I want to tell you about."

He went on to tell me of the career of his old dog. Being a musician, he worked anti-social hours and it became his habit to while away sunny afternoons exercising the dog on Box Hill. This he did by throwing a ball off the top of the hill, at its steepest part, for the dog to retrieve. She became so obsessed with this that she grew increasingly fit and developed thigh muscles that would have flattered a rugby league forward.

An acquaintance of Mr X mentioned that she should be fit enough to race and accordingly arranged to take them to a disreputable flapping track. Here, the guide dog swapped her harness for a coloured jacket and learned to come out of the traps and race. Apparently, she even won a few times.

Some time later, Mr X got a job as a resident musician at a country club. He was provided with a cottage in the grounds, which the dog was free to explore at will. Soon, he and the dog began to lead a life that met with the approval of them both. After he finished work each night, it became habitual for the other musicians to return for late drinks and a jam session. While they played, the back door would be left open and the dog would spend the night catching and retrieving rabbits. This continued until, one night, a drunken guest, returning by car, ran her over and she died instantly.

"I thought you'd like to know what happened," Mr X said quietly. "She was one hell of a dog, and there'll never be another one like her. But, by God, she had a full life."

It was a sad ending, but I can't help thinking that she

did more than most dogs ever get to do, and she gave a lot of pleasure to her owner. Old Hugh, who puppy-walked her, is long dead now, I'm no longer with the Guide Dogs, and there are no more clandestine, shaggy-haired Lurchers tucked away on the puppy-walking scheme to avoid recovery by an irate Scottish poacher. A bit of a pity, wouldn't you say?

While You're Here . . .

Andrew Edney, vet

It was a dark and stormy night, and I was rushing to an emergency call. It was very late and I was trying to marshal my thoughts on what I might encounter. It was then that I drove my car through a brick wall!

It could have happened to anyone. Even though I was on a road that I drove along every day, I had mistakenly thought a T-junction was a crossroads (I was not the first – and I will not be the last – to do this). By the time I came to rest, it was.

I was as new to driving as I was to the veterinary profession, and it was in the days before seat belts were a legal requirement. I looked up to see the wall getting bigger very rapidly, and managed to steer the part of the car I was in through a large gate attached to the wall. The rest of the vehicle knocked the wall down. My chest hit the steering wheel and pushed the steering column through the windscreen just before my head did the same.

By some miracle, I was fortunate enough to emerge from the now wedge-shaped Morris 1000 with superficial – but very bloody – cuts to my face (a little blood looks like a lot of blood). However, what really hurt was the Winchester (a heavy, two-litre glass bottle) of sulphamezathine solution, which had hit me on the head as the contents of the boot were projected into the car. Vets of my vintage will know that 'sulphamez' contained a dye called Brilliant Green.

I pulled myself from the wreckage and made my way to the house on the property I had invaded. It bore a striking resemblance to the Bates Motel on a bad night. I tapped tentatively on the door, which eventually opened to reveal a rather excitable lady from northern Europe. She let out a fearsome shriek as she saw this person covered in blood and brilliant green sulphamez, with fragments of windscreen glass forming a halo around his head, who uttered, "I've had a bit of an accident. Can I use your telephone, please?"

At this point, her husband shouted from upstairs to enquire what was going on. On being appraised of the situation, he uttered the memorable words: "He hasn't damaged the wall, has he?"

They allowed me to telephone the garage to recover the car (it was a write-off) and my boss to deal with the emergency call-out. The principal of our practice seemed to be the only person concerned with my state of health.

After an extensive wash, my face assumed a pale-grey colour. I set about making arrangements to get home. It was at this time that it became clear to my new acquaintances that I was a vet. It was then that I heard my first and worst 'while you're here' request.

"Oh, we have been thinking of getting a vet in to look at the dog," the lady of the house said. Well, I don't dislike German Shepherd Dogs, but this one was hard work. My slightly colourful, bizarre appearance did not help.

The dog had the full set of canine aggressions, as well as anal furunculosis and a chronic ear problem. Worst of all, the owners were afraid of him.

The lesson learned from this was that when you hear the words 'while you're here… will you…?' it will be something tricky and will take twice as long as the time you had allowed for the visit.

A year or so later, a three-ton army truck knocked

down 'my' wall. By chance, I happened to be passing by soon afterwards. I stopped and found an army corporal driver looking very pale as he sat rigid in his seat. "Brakes failed, didn't they mate!" he stuttered.

Just as I was about to relate my experiences of the year before, the excitable Russian lady appeared. She saw the wreckage, the collapsed wall, and me standing alongside. As she was about to launch into attack mode on me, I drew her attention to the fact that I was but a passer-by and it was the military gent who was responsible on this occasion. She then tore into him, saying he ought to be ashamed of himself, as it was broad daylight, whereas with me it had been a "night not fit for the dog".

There is a roundabout there now.

I HATE VETS! ESPECIALLY GREEN ONES.!

Water Baby

Barbara Swann, Working Collie specialist

With a deep interest in industrial architecture, I took a friend and Lady the collie to visit the first iron bridge built over the River Severn at Ironbridge.

Lady was obsessed by water, and never thinking she would jump from the ultra-steep high bank, I was caught by surprise when she landed in the water. There were extremely dangerous currents and I was out of my mind, as there was no way I could get her out.

The bank was steeply sloped around six feet to the river with fine, gritty material. The rescue must have been an odd sight. Fortunately, Lady had a rounded leather collar on and I had a shepherd's crook. I lay face down on the edge, some six feet above her, while my friend held on to my feet and legs. Edging down the slope slightly, I was able to hook the crook under the collar and my friend was able to pull me plus the dog back to terra firma.

All her life, Lady could smell water before I could see it, and was always indulging in her passion. I often had to pull her out of canals that she couldn't manage to clamber out of.

Grub Robber

Audrey Plum, volunteer at Guide Dogs and Dogs for the Disabled

It was a lovely summer's day way back in the mid-70s, and the town streets were crowded with shoppers. A guide dog owner was walking with her dog in one direction, and, coming towards her on the same side of the road but in the opposite direction was a family. A mother had a child of about three years of age in a pushchair, enjoying a newly purchased ice-cream. The guide dog levelled with the child, and, without breaking step, snatched the cornet.

Normally, guide dog owners can tell what the dog is doing by the different feelings in the handle of the harness, but, on this occasion, the owner didn't feel a thing. The dog couldn't have dropped the cornet either, because absolutely nothing was felt along the harness – he just kept going at his normal pace.

Chaos rained down upon this unfortunate guide dog

owner only a few moments later. She didn't know what was happening to her. All the family had gathered round her, shouting in a foreign tongue, and she was quite frightened because she had absolutely no idea what they were shouting about. Eventually, an English-speaking shopper came to her assistance and explained what had happened.

The only thing this lady could do was to give the child some money to buy another ice-cream cornet. In the end, calm was restored and the family went on, presumably pacifying the child with another ice-cream.

A similar theft by a guide dog happened along the same lines. The owner didn't know what had happened, and neither did the unfortunate shopper who had half a pound of butter stolen from her open basket. She must have thought she had left the butter on the counter after paying for it.

I wonder if guide dogs do such naughty things these days?

No Riff At RAF

Clive Gilmore, retired RAF police dog handler and instructor

Although I have been with dogs since my earliest recollection, there has always been a strong affinity with all animals. After leaving school, I worked on my stepfather's dairy farm and was fascinated by the work of the farm dogs. As a teenager, I bought my very own dog, a yellow Labrador bitch, and later joined my local dog training society.

In early 1953, at the age of 18, I joined the Royal Air Force, where I qualified as a RAF police dog handler. The five years I spent in the service was an enormous benefit to me, gaining experience in animal husbandry and training. Two years of this period was spent in charge of the quarantine and isolation section, a unit that had about 60 dogs and a staff of kennel maids. The last two years of my service was on instructional duties in Germany, turning RAF police dogs and handlers into efficient working teams for operational duties.

These years in the RAF encouraged me to look for employment with working dogs when I left the service. Fortunately, not long after completing my service engagement, a vacancy occurred for a civilian instructional officer at the RAF police dog school. I applied and was successful at turning what started as a hobby into a profession. The professionalism and enthusiasm of the staff at the dog training establishment was infectious to any newcomer.

There were numerous, memorable occasions over my 35 years – royal visits, royal tournaments, visiting foreign dignitaries, visits to RAF stations in the near and far-east, and many judging appointments in the UK and Germany.

Along with the ups, there was the occasional down. One tragic incident struck into the heart of the RAF police dog world in 1957. On 5 March, an RAF transport plane crashed soon after leaving Abingdon in Oxfordshire. On board, there were nine RAF handlers and their dogs on their way to a posting in Cyprus. They all lost their lives. In total, 17 passengers and two civilians on the ground also died. The pilot, co-pilot and one other officer were the only three to escape. Amazingly, this flight had been arranged and postponed six times and then flew on the fatal seventh. An ill-fated loss of men, and dogs.

How did the RAF obtain the large number of dogs (at that time, all German Shepherds) they needed? By two sources – their own breeding programme and the gift dog scheme. The breeding programme produced many suitable dogs, but, by 1950, so many young adult dogs and bitches were being acquired from the public as unconditional gifts that the breeding plan was discontinued.

The thousands of dogs donated by the public all kept their original names. If I was to select two unusual names from the many dogs that I had contact with, they would have to be Xhonophone (RAF-bred), and Boomerang (a gift dog). Fortunately, both names were shortened for training purposes to become Phonie and Boo.

It was not until 1970 that the RAF police started recruiting other breeds into the service, when search programmes were introduced for the detection of drugs, firearms and explosives, and breeds from the gundog varieties were tried with great success.

The privilege of working with the RAF police and their dogs for 40 years, and the many lifetime friendships that were formed, made it a job in a million and the wonderful memories will stay with me forever.

Finally, I would like to close with the RAF police dog school motto: "Don't punish your dog, train it!"

Do You Believe In Ghosts?

Bob Haynes, former police dog handler

My story starts back in the mid-1960s. I was a young policeman working in Coventry. As was the custom in those days, I was being shown around the various beats before being allowed out on my own.

One night, I was working the beat in the Wyken area of Coventry, and was being shown around by a long-serving bobby, who was a mine of local information. He took me through the local churchyard and showed me "the pirate's grave". This was an extremely old and weathered tombstone on which could still be seen a carved skull and crossbones.

My guide explained that no one really knew how this

stone came to be in place and that it was a local mystery – especially when Coventry is about as far from the sea as it is possible to get.

He went on to say that, over the years, a number of people had experienced strange happenings in the churchyard – all attributed to the ghost of the pirate who was believed to be buried there. When I pressed him for more details, it became clear that he did not know anyone who had experienced them, but lots of people who knew other people who had!

I relegated this information to the back of my mind and thought little of it.

My story now jumps forward to the mid-1980s when I was a dog handler, still working in Coventry. I was very fortunate to have a dog, who, even at that time, was described as an 'old-fashioned police dog'. This dog, who was named Flint, feared nothing and would fight anything. When I was with him, I was confident of dealing with any hostile situation that presented itself.

One particular summer's night, Flint and I were called to the Wyken area, where a prowler had been disturbed in someone's rear garden. Unfortunately, because of commitments on the other side of the city, it took us longer to get to the scene than I would have liked. Because of our late arrival, I was informed that officers had already searched the surrounding area but had found nothing. These officers were now clearing from the scene. Nevertheless, I decided to search the area with Flint, just in case there was still someone about.

After about 15 minutes, the course of our search had taken us into the grounds of the local church. It was still light, and I decided to wait at the side of the church and just look out across a flat, lawned area, which led out to an open field. Flint was lying down at my side.

After some minutes of daydreaming about the end of the shift, I suddenly became aware of a change in Flint's manner. He had stood up in an aggressive stance, staring out across the lawn – but there was no one at all in his line of sight. Looking back at him, I was shocked to see that every hair on his body was standing out straight.

He started to snarl in the most aggressive manner I had ever heard. Remember, this was a naturally aggressive dog, who I had seen, on numerous occasions, showing aggression towards criminals that he had found, but never had I seen him behave like this. I was totally perplexed, as I did not know what was causing him to behave this way.

Flint started to take very stilted steps forward and then suddenly he leapt forward and upwards in an attack. He jumped up to about chest height and forward just a few feet, as if attacking a man in front of us. I heard his jaws crash together in a biting action. Then, to my horror, the dog let out a pitiful squeal, fell to the ground, crawled back to me in a totally cowed manner and stayed behind me.

YO HO HO AND A BOTTLE OF RUM!!

To say I was astounded would be an understatement. This was a dog who would take on any armed criminal without a second thought. Something had totally terrified him, but I was sure that no one was there.

Deciding that discretion is the better part of valour, I took the dog and myself away from the churchyard and back to the station.

At the station the dog was his normal self as if nothing had happened. He suffered no other effects from his experience at all.

I thought long and hard about this experience. There is no doubt that Flint had been terrified by what had happened. I was sure that there was no other person there at the time, and if there had been, they would not have frightened a dog like Flint.

I then started to think about the night back in the 1960s when I was told about the pirate's grave and the strange happenings in the churchyard – the same churchyard where Flint and I had our unnerving experience. Had Flint seen something that I could not see? Had he attempted to defend me against what he believed to be an assailant? Had Flint seen the pirate's ghost? Of course, we will never know, but I know what I think, and the answer to the question posed at the beginning of this story is… yes!

Basic Instinct

Harold Jennings, guide dog owner

I have been a guide dog owner for more than 30 years. During that time, there have been numerous occasions when my dogs have shown exceptional skill and initiative.

My first guide dog was Ivor. We used to take our Dutch street organ to many traction-engine rallies, where Ivor would find his way, not only back to our organ, but to those owned by friends, and, of course, to the beer tent.

My second dog was Harvey. Two years before he retired, we bought a motor caravan. Harvey soon became adept at finding the van on the sites that we used to visit, and he could also find the toilet block.

Luke, my third dog, also worked well on caravan sites. On one occasion, he treated a heap of horse manure on the pavement as an off-curb obstacle, and took the appropriate avoiding action.

All my dogs have been very good at finding the many houses, schools etc. that I have had to visit during my career as a piano tuner. They have been able to find locations from the opposite side of streets.

Last year, I took part in a project that entailed a number of lengthy train journeys on routes to unfamiliar stations. Wesley, my current dog, amazed me by the way that he coped with the long days and the many changes of trains that had to be made on someof the trips.

Wuthering Heights

Neil Ewart, Guide Dogs staff member

Many years ago, I regularly competed in working trials with a couple of almost totally black German Shepherd Dogs – and one was called Heathcliff.

The sendaway exercise involves pointing your dog in a direction indicated by the judge and sending him to a certain point some distance away.

It was a misty afternoon in late autumn. Off went Heathcliff, actually disappearing over the brow of a hill, but still roughly where he was supposed to go. The judge instructed me to call the dog back.

Now came that moment. Stood on a hillside in deepest Yorkshire, I cupped my hands and yelled, "Heathcliff!" Cathy would have been most impressed. Back came my hero and the exercise was over.

The judge came up to me and asked, in a very broad Yorkshire accent, where I had found the name

Heathcliff. His steward rounded on him. "Don't you know? Have you never read *Lorna Doone!*"

At the same trials, I witnessed one of the best sendaways ever. A male Dobermann was put in position and was sent off. He streaked up the hill in a perfect straight line until confronted by a substantial stone wall, where he skidded to a halt. On his return, I complimented his handler and asked how he had trained the dog so well. "There was no training involved," he replied. "No one noticed, but he was chasing a ruddy seagull!"

Safety Precautions

Maurice Hall, former Guide Dogs trainer

The smart young university lecturer marched up to the lectern with his guide dog, and, in the usual way, removed the harness to enable his trusted friend and guide to relax and sleep through the lecture. As always, the dog had been taken for a run in the park prior to entering the theatre, so all was well.

It usually took a few minutes for the students to settle. Today was different – there was total silence. In fact, it could be described as a deathly hush! Then came the whispers, and then the giggles, leading to hysteria!

Unknown to the owner, the very caring guide dog had played his part in keeping the park clear of litter. He had retrieved a condom, which was still in his mouth. It was carefully removed, and the lecturer thanked the students present for "taking the necessary precautions" during their extramural studies!

Shock Treatment

Audrey Plum, volunteer at Guide Dogs and Dogs for the Disabled

It was a pleasant day for dog walking. One of Enfield's Dog Training Club members (Gloria) took her two dogs to a wide open space to let them have a jolly good romp and run about. Then, from nowhere, appeared a dog intent on a fight, who set about one of Gloria's dogs.

Gloria was alone and couldn't call for assistance, so what was she to do? In a flash, she had a brilliant idea. With her left hand, she grabbed the ferocious dog's tail and lifted him off his back feet; with two of her right-hand fingers set like a gun, she inserted them into the dog's anus! The dog stopped in his tracks, let go of his quarry, and fled.

Rash(er) Decision

Jenny Moir, head of PR, Hearing Dogs for Deaf People

Daisy's recipient, Vonnie, was cooking bacon one day and went out of the kitchen. She didn't realise that the bacon was burning, which had set off the smoke alarm, but Daisy, a tiny Yorkshire Terrier cross, went to find her, scrabbled at her, and then lay down to indicate danger.

A neighbour, who had heard the alarm, came and explained the situation to Vonnie, who then turned the smoke alarm off. What she hadn't realised was that the alarm was connected to the central fire station in Exeter. About five minutes later, little Daisy was scrabbling at Vonnie again. This time she led her to the window, and when Vonnie looked out, she saw two fire engines and 12 firefighters in her garden!

The Nose Of A Dobe

Mike Mullan, dog trainer and Kennel Club member

It was a damp, misty November evening. I was returning home after an evening's dog training with my four-year-old Dobermann, Barbie.

As I travelled down the road, I noticed that there were people with torches walking about the army firing ranges and it was obvious that they were searching for something or someone.

As I came out of an S-bend, I passed two parked police cars. Perhaps they were searching for a missing child, or perhaps a patient from the nearby hospital for the mentally ill, I thought.

I decided to turn around, and went back to where the cars were parked. A policeman immediately appeared to be expecting me and said, "Good evening, sir. Thank you for turning out so promptly."

After a few explanations, it was clear that he had mistaken me for a vet, who had been called out to despatch a deer that had recently been hit by a car. The officer went on to say that when he arrived, the deer was nowhere in sight. However, it seemed that it had escaped on to army land, and the police were concerned that it may find its way back on to the road network and cause another accident.

By now it was about 10.15pm and I asked whether I could be of any assistance, as I had a dog in my car who was capable of quartering the ground – if the deer was still around, Barbie would quickly find it. They accepted the offer, as the local police dogs were employed elsewhere that night.

When I lifted the tailgate of my car to reveal one rather large, black-and-tan Dobermann (she was 27 inches at the shoulder), an officer backed off, saying,

"Sorry, mate, no way. That dog will attack or eat the deer – let alone us!" I explained again that Barbie was completely under control and was trained to track – she would never hurt anything she found. All she would do ·is... bark!

Eventually, an officer decided to give her a go, as they had already searched for an hour and had found nothing.

I took Barbie to the place where the deer had lain after the accident. As I set Barbie up, a policeman asked, "Are you sure the dog will not hurt the deer?" I reassured him again, steadied Barbie, showed her the site, let her take the scent, and then commanded her, "Go seek!"

Barbie set off like a train. She went in a straight line for a dozen yards, then veered right, then again headed off in a straight line, followed by a sharp left turn, heading rapidly towards a rather worried policeman.

My heart sank. "How could she let me down like this?" I thought. "She's going straight to that copper. What a fool I am going to look!" Of course, I should have known better. How many times have I said to other handlers, "Trust your dog, do not interfere. The dog knows best – he's using his nose."

Of course, that was what Barbie was doing. She had absolutely no interest in the policeman, for she stopped short of him and started to bark.

Another alarmed policeman arrived, asking if his mate was safe! Of course he was. Barbie had found the poor deer, still alive but in a terrible condition. Fortunately, the vet arrived at that moment and put the animal out of its misery.

The police had been a few feet away from it and must have passed close by at least six times. If Barbie had not found the deer, it probably would have lain there in agony all night.

I was so proud of Barbie and I still miss her so much...

Deepest Sleep

Andrew Edney, vet

Most of the town where I practised was respectable, well behaved and perhaps a touch boring. However, there was a small region to the north-east, which you only visited if you had to. It was here that I learned one of the most chilling lessons of my career.

The dog I visited on regular intervals to this area was mainly German Shepherd, with a number of genes derived from individuals of varying degrees of unpleasantness. He had not had a kindly upbringing and was one of those individuals who 'did not like men'. In his three years' existence, he had not benefited from socialisation. He particularly did not like vets who came to his fourth-floor flat to inspect his failing skin and smelly ears. Worst of all, the dog's owner was not the alpha individual in the territory she occupied with this fearsome GSD cross.

Having done my best to examine the dog and to apply various substances to the inflamed areas, the owner uttered words that sounded quite decisive. She yelled across the room that she was "fed up with all this" and she "wanted the dog put to sleep". I knew it would be fruitless to try countering this by suggesting dog training classes or any form of schooling. So, I opened my black bag, took out a large syringe, and filled it with the concentrated barbiturate solution we used to dispatch animals, inducing anaesthesia to the point of no return.

I managed to secure the dog's biting regions with my trusty old pyjama cord, forming a muzzle. Using a modified wrestling manoeuvre, I was ready to inject. As I was on the point of ending the dog's life, the owner casually asked when I would see the dog again for his usual check-up.

"But you said…!" I began to stutter until I realised that she wanted me to anaesthetise the dog and not kill him. The lesson I learned was that, where you use euphemisms for killing, you need to make absolutely sure that it is what is required. You can do this by getting the owner to sign a consent form but another way is to discuss what is going to happen afterwards with respect to the disposal of the body.

I left the practice soon after that, and, as far as I know, the dog may have lived another 10 to 15 years. But I doubt it.

Fizzical Farce

Jenny Moir, head of PR, Hearing Dogs for Deaf People

Soon after mongrel Fizz had been placed with her recipient, Tracey, they were in a local shop. Fizz had her headcollar on, but was fussing with it. As she was doing this, she rubbed between another lady's legs. This lady turned round and slapped Tracey's husband as she thought he had been touching her up!

Another time, Tracey and Fizz were standing outside a shop when a woman tried to give Tracey £5 "for the dog"!

I'VE GOT TO BE WORTH MORE THAN A FIVER!!

The Lucky Lurcher

Steve Dean, vet

Lucky is a Lurcher. How she came to be called Lucky will become clear as this tale unfolds.

One Sunday lunchtime, my wife and I were driving along the M25, heading towards a party at a friend's new veterinary surgery. It was a sunny day and all was proceeding as planned, except we were late – but that is quite normal for a vet (at least, this one).

We were in the middle lane, travelling at precisely 70 mph, of course, when a vision of horror filled the windscreen. There was a dog in the outside lane, clearly distressed and in serious danger of being killed. Through pure reflex, we headed for the hard shoulder, brakes full on, the ABS system working overtime, and then reversed back up the hard shoulder, expecting to find a grisly scene and a very dead dog.

In the few seconds the dog had been in view, as we had flashed past, her distress and fear were obvious, as were two broken fore-legs, snapped in mid-shaft between elbow and wrist. I was on auto-pilot and high on adrenaline as I leapt from the car. I do not remember, but apparently I told my wife to stay put and not do anything silly – in fact, she said she was told to sit and stay! All pretty daft, considering what happened next.

Glancing to the middle of the road, I saw that Lucky had been sensible enough to scrabble to the central reservation and had amazingly survived so far. To my right, the M25 was miraculously empty of cars, so, without a further moment of thought, I sprinted across to her.

As I approached, Lucky came close to being spooked, and her body language suggested she might try to run away from me. A momentary vision flashed through my mind of what her flight into the other carriageway would do. So I ran to the centre a few yards away from this poor animal.

Meanwhile, behind us, the traffic was fiercely flowing; the lull that had permitted my sprint to the centre was over. On the other side, the carriageway was also busy, and cars flashed by our precarious position. It was at this point that reality kicked in and I realised that Lucky and I were both in serious danger. There was no obvious way out, so there I was, edging towards a frightened dog, who was probably in serious pain, with traffic buzzing by on both sides. Lucky was on the far side of the crash barriers, on the verge of running at any minute. I was speaking to her, trying to sound calm and friendly – frankly not an easy task when you are scared witless.

In the end, my fingertips were in reach of her collar but I could not quite grab it securely. At this point, I felt slightly foolish, balancing on my stomach, while leaning over a crash barrier with cars whizzing just feet from my rear end and my head.

Looking up, I saw a police car, blue lights flashing and siren singing, coming down the fast lane on the opposite side of the M25. I saw the police officer clearly, and he saw me too. There was no difficulty reading his lips either as he said, "What the hell is that *$!?*%* idiot doing?" Not surprisingly, the police car also headed for the hard shoulder and reversed back towards Lucky and me, much faster and with a lot more skill than I had achieved earlier.

One policeman leapt from the car and the other drove off, blue lights still flashing. Now, it is amazing to say this, but, for the second time that day, the traffic on the M25 paused for a short while, this time on the other carriageway. The officer sprinted towards me but I shouted a warning to him, as I saw Lucky was on the verge of bolting again. In a split second, he changed his trajectory to arrive at the central reservation several yards away from us.

Heavens be praised that Lucky, in moving away from him, gave me just the opportunity I needed to get three fingers under her collar. It may have been fear or determination – who knows? – but these three fingers were locked around the collar, and wild horses could not have parted me and that dog from that moment on.

As the policeman approached, with an amazing burst of strength, I lifted Lucky over the barrier and into my arms. I turned to the officer and said, "It's okay, I am a vet." Without batting an eyelid, he replied, "Good sir, then you look after the dog and leave the motorway to me!"

I stood still as ordered, except my knees were knocking – either with exertion or fear. Soon the other policeman appeared, now on our carriageway, in the centre lane, lights flashing, right arm waving down traffic.

"Now sir, please wait until all three lanes of traffic have entirely stopped, and be careful of the nutters – there are always nutters," said my guardian angel. Sure enough, as the three lanes of traffic came to a halt behind a very obvious police vehicle, two cars flashed by in the fast lane, totally oblivious to the situation at hand. As I stood on the central reservation, clutching Lucky, I thought the officer was right – there are always nutters and the nuttiest of them all was standing right next to him.

He turned to me and said, "Right sir, now I think we will walk across slowly," as if I could do anything else on my shaking limbs. It is quite awesome walking across three lanes of the M25 with several hundred cars standing motionless, waiting impatiently.

Once we had gained the comparative safety of the hard shoulder, the police took more interest in my injured charge. I still had a firm grip on Lucky, as she was still in some distress – though amazingly co-operative. Not once had she tried to bite me, despite the pain she must have been in. We had a police escort as far as the surgery, and so the next part of this tale begins.

Please imagine a gathering of friends and potential clients drinking fine wine and nibbling canapés. Enter stage left, the wife of a veterinary friend with some tale about her husband – a known joker and wind-up merchant – rescuing a dog from the clutches of the M25. So there was much laughter and cries of "Come back tomorrow when we are open for business". Then enter stage left, the veterinary friend clutching a Lurcher, trousers covered in blood, looking somewhat stressed.

So Lucky was the first patient seen in this brand new surgery. The veterinary machine sprung into action. We put splints on her limbs, gave her some pain relief, and considered our next move. Now, please bear in mind

that I had just risked life and limb for this dog. We were now faced with a dog with no owner, compound fractures to both forelimbs, and an uncertain future. The surgery and after-care would be expensive, and even if money could be found, who would look after our new little friend during her recovery and afterwards?

Now call me devious, but when my wife came to find out how Lucky was, I explained our dilemma. "What if nobody claims her?" she asked. "Well, we may have to put her down." I replied. Such blackmail was guaranteed to succeed. "Well, surely we could look after her," said my wife. Bingo! We immediately started planning the operations to repair Lucky's fractured limbs for the next day. My wife looked slightly bemused, wondering if perhaps she had been outflanked.

So we repaired Lucky's legs. They took a little time to heal, but she was fine in the end and lived in a very good home with two other Lurchers. Oh, and by the way, we called her Lucky because it rhymed with 'plucky'.

Learning The Hard Way

Roger Haywood, ex-inspector of the West Midlands police dog section

As a child, I had been brought up to love dogs. My father bred Fox Terriers and Staffordshire Bull Terriers, but I always wanted to own a German Shepherd Dog that I could take to training classes.

My father made me a deal. "Pass your 11-plus to go to grammar school and you can have a GSD." With this as an incentive, I did pass and Kim was the commencement of my fascination with this wonderful breed.

After National Service in the Navy, I joined

Birmingham City police in 1957. As soon as I had completed my probationary period, I applied to be considered for training as a police dog handler. Despite my enthusiasm, it took me until 1962 before I was eventually accepted.

One very cold morning in December 1962, I reported to the police dog training school at Harbourne (Birmingham), to start my career as a handler. I was introduced to the other members of the course by Sergeant Alan Hutchinson, the instructor. He informed us that our first duty was to exercise the trained police dogs who were being kennelled at Harbourne while their handlers were taking time off. We all went into the kennel block, and I was handed a lead and told to go and walk a dog in kennel six, named Andy.

Imagine my surprise when I found Andy – he wasn't a GSD, but a yellow Labrador!

I spoke to him through the door, and he responded by wagging his tail. I showed him the lead, and he jumped up at the kennel door, with his tail wagging even faster. I had made a friend.

I slowly opened the kennel and carefully stepped inside, making sure that Andy did not bolt past me. I turned towards him and he promptly sank his teeth into my left leg!

I shot out of the kennel, nursing a very painful leg, and immediately reported the incident to Sgt Hutchinson. I expected some sympathy but did I get it? Oh, no! I was told that I had probably upset Andy in some way. "You have got to take some biscuits in with you, as Labradors are very partial to them. In fact, Andy will do anything for one."

Now in possession of the first golden rule of handling Labradors, I returned to kennel six with a handful of biscuits. Andy stood, wagging his tail. I showed him the biscuits and his wagging increased. Then, to my surprise, he sat up on his tail in a perfect begging position. Cautiously, I slowly opened the kennel door and quickly gave him a biscuit. It went down in one gulp and he immediately adopted the begging stance again. The second biscuit rapidly disappeared, followed by a third. Now, I was back inside the kennel, standing very gingerly in front of Andy, who still only had eyes for the remaining biscuits.

I should have known better but this was, after all, my first day! Determined to make friends, I continued until my supply of biscuits expired. I patted him on the head and told him that he was a good boy.

"Sorry, Andy," I said, "No more," showing him my empty hands. He promptly showed his appreciation by sinking his teeth into my right leg!

I limped back to Sgt Hutchinson to be informed it must have been my fault. I had obviously upset Andy by teasing him with the biscuits.

Fortunately, on this occasion, Sgt Hutchinson took the time to instruct me how to use biscuits to entice Andy to have his lead clipped on to his collar. Once out of the kennel, all Andy wanted to do was drag me on an inspection tour of the local trees.

It wasn't until some time later that I discovered that introducing recruit dog handlers to the likes of Andy was considered an 'essential' part of our experiences.

Over a period of time, I did get to know Andy, and his handler, PC Jim Fox, better.

I certainly learnt that there were a lot of criminals in the Birmingham area who would verify that one particular Labrador, Andy, had a hard mouth and a full set of sharp teeth.

Itsy Bitsy Spider

Trevor Turner, vet and author

A young Labrador was brought in to an emergency Sunday-morning clinic by a worried owner. The dog was fine but the owner was sure he had seen the Lab playing with his two-year-old daughter's toy plastic spider the evening before.

The spider could no longer be found. Could the dog have eaten it?

"How big was it?" I asked.

"Oh, the body is about an inch to an inch-and-a-half across."

Careful examination revealed nothing abnormal. There was no vomiting and the dog had defecated on the way to the surgery. Careful abdominal palpation revealed no pain.

"Can't you X-ray him?" asked the owner.

"I can," I replied, "but it is unlikely to be of value, since plastic does not show up on X-rays. I suggest you keep a careful eye on the dog and let us know if he loses his appetite, vomits, strains to pass motion, etc. etc."

The owner came into a routine surgery about five days later, reporting that the daughter had not found her favourite spider and would I check the dog again? Same routine, same outcome, same advice.

My next contact was about two years later. Again, a Sunday. The duty veterinary surgeon had been treating the dog for the previous few days for vomiting and straining.

He had originally diagnosed chronic constipation but the worried owner had come in on the Sunday morning because the Lab had deteriorated.

I was called by my colleague following an emergency laparatomy. A green and black object had been removed from the small intestine. What did I think it was? After careful examination, I came to the conclusion that it was the heavily acid-etched body of a toy spider.

AM I GLAD TO SEE YOU!!

Clearly the owner was right, and it had resided in the stomach, subject to digestive juices, for two years before deciding to take the journey through the bowel. The dog made an uneventful recovery.

Bedside Manner

Robert Killick, canine author, columnist, and legend!

A couple of years ago, I was in hospital for a week. In the next bed was an old man in his mid-90s. He lay absolutely still, showing no signs of life except his gentle breathing. His eyes were open but he didn't respond to anything. His family sat with him all day, trying to stimulate him.

One morning, a great grandson, who was about seven years of age, came in carrying the old man's Jack Russell. You know the sort of dog – short, crooked legs and full of fun. The boy put the dog on the bed and he positively leapt on the old fellow, tail whirring like a helicopter blade. He licked the old man's face furiously.

After a few seconds, the man lifted both arms to stroke the dog – the first movement he'd made in weeks. Then he smiled and gently spoke the dog's name. The following day, the old chap was sitting up and speaking animatedly to anyone who would listen. The dog visited every day, and the old fellow looked progressively better each time.

Talent Beyond Belief

Steve Burnell, guide dog owner

Some years ago, my wife, two friends and I visited a large garden that was open to the public. We had with us my own guide dog and my friend's guide dog. We checked at the entrance that guide dogs were allowed – they were. However, while we were admiring an immaculate flowerbed, the owner's elderly wife came rushing up to announce that no dogs were allowed. When we explained that they were guide dogs, her attitude changed completely and she called her husband over to see the dogs.

During the time that we were deep in conversation, my German Shepherd Dog had been happily eating large amounts of grass. The inevitable result was that the dog started the long, drawn-out process of bringing up the grass she had swallowed on to the immaculate flowerbed in full view of the owner and his wife. Not having anything suitable for the dog to be sick on to, my wife grabbed the only piece of paper she had available – the plan of the gardens.

So there stood my dog, head down, about to be sick on to the plan of the gardens. Whereupon the owner's wife announced in sheer amazement, "Oh look, darling, aren't they wonderful – that dog can even read the map!"

Canine Global Positioning System

Maurice Hall, former Guide Dogs trainer

Carol Mudge and her black Labrador guide dog, Bess, visited a friend by taxi. The next time, they used the bus, with very clear instructions on how to continue on foot.

Unfortunately, Carol was let off the bus at the wrong stop. After some ten minutes, it was becoming apparent that perhaps something was not quite right. Another ten minutes elapsed, and it was now obvious that they were on the wrong route, and there were no other pedestrians around for information. It was left to Bess to solve the problem. About 25 minutes later, Bess turned very determinedly into an unfamiliar driveway and very proudly led her owner up to the front door. They had arrived! A very amused Carol could not describe the route taken but was very proud of her Bess!

Talk To The Animals

Jenny Moir, head of PR, Hearing Dogs for Deaf People

This happened during the filming of *Pet Rescue* with Didi, a Papillon, her recipient, Norma, and presenter Wendy Turner Webster.

They were all outside Asda, waiting to go in and do some filming of the dog in the supermarket. A lady came up, and, looking down at Didi, started asking questions. "Isn't he lovely? How old is he?" and so on.

Our trainer interrupted the lady, and, pointing to Norma, said, "She is deaf, but if you speak slowly and clearly so she can read your lips, she will be able to understand what you are saying." With this, the lady promptly knelt on the floor, and, looking straight into Didi's face, said "Hello, how old are you then?"

Breathe In . . .

Viv Alemi, vet

When guide dog Lace came in for her routine health checks, she would hold her breath when her chest was being examined, making it almost impossible to check her lungs properly.

Clarity Disparity

Val Strong, training manager, Support Dogs

I was arranging to visit a member of the public regarding a problem she had with her male entire German Shepherd Dog.

I explained that, as the dog was extremely aggressive towards strangers, I would like her to put him in the back garden prior to my arrival to minimise any confrontation at the front door.

I arrived at the house, opened the front gate and proceeded towards the front door. As I was about to ring the doorbell, I heard a roar from behind and turned to see the GSD preparing to launch an attack.

The lady had indeed put the dog in the back garden, but had failed to explain that there was not a gate to prevent the dog getting into the front garden!

Thankfully, she opened the door just in time for me to get in before the dog hit the closing door in a rage.

Another amusing anecdote concerns a dog trained to go into the post office for her disabled owner. The four-legged helper was complained about by another customer, who was heard to say, "Excuse me, but I was in front of the dog!"

Down Memory Lane

Roy Bee, guide dog owner

I was given my first guide dog, Betsy, on my 29th birthday. Six months after qualifying I did a course of telephony at the RNIB (Royal National Institute for the Blind), where, in those days, dogs were not allowed. Betsy had to be put on a train back to Bolton.

Regulations stated that dogs travelling in a guard's van must be muzzled. Poor Betsy walked along the station platform doing her utmost to remove this attachment by rubbing the side of her head on the floor. She was most unhappy, but the good thing was that, as soon as the guard saw her, he said, "We'll have that bloody thing off for a start."

After completing the course at the RNIB and being reunited with Betsy, one of the tutors invited my wife and myself to lunch, which was very nice. It would have been even nicer if we'd had a pudding – but Betsy got there first. Occurrences like this were to become a regular thing throughout Betsy's career and carried on into retirement, causing the oft-used expression "Oh, Betsy!"

My second period of training was at Leamington Spa with Warren. It is the greatest pity that there are not more human beings in this world that have the same attitude towards life that Warren had. He couldn't understand why people had to shout at him or anyone else. I once caught him trying to rub noses with a guinea pig. Cats were allowed the run of the garden, and the budgie used to land on his back, but he never made any attempt to harm the bird.

It is a long time ago, but I still find it difficult to talk about the sudden death of my third dog. Dogs are sick from time to time, particularly Labradors. Perrin was sick on Sunday afternoon and had to be put to sleep on the following Tuesday. I am not ashamed to say that I shed tears that day. It was so sudden. Only a few months previously, the vet had congratulated me on Perrin's well-being. My last memory of him was when he went with the nurse, wagging his tail. I never saw him again.

Naomi (guide dog number four) suffered with epilepsy, but I was assured that she would never have a fit while in harness. Going to work one morning, we approached a driveway that she seemed anxious to cross, but as soon as she reached what she must have considered safety, poor Naomi sank to the floor. I realised that she was having a fit and promptly squatted down beside her and talked to her.

After a while, someone called Paul from the nearby car sales establishment came to find out what the problem was and to see if he could help. When I explained the situation, he said, "Right, tell me what you need doing." I said that my problem was that I had to get to work to sort things out from there. Paul picked her up and off we went. When we arrived at the office, he carried her in and made sure that we were okay. Forever after that, Naomi looked for Paul every time we went by his place.

My present partner behaves quite differently from his predecessors, which is not altogether surprising, as they were all Labradors and Corky is a Standard Poodle. Getting him was just what I needed. It stopped me from becoming complacent, which can happen if you work only with one breed of dog.

To illustrate the breed difference, Corky and I were out walking one day when we both realised that there was rather a large machine coming towards us on the pavement. Corky stopped and so did the road-sweeping machine.

As we got close by, Corky considered whether it was safe to go. A voice said, "There's enough room to get by", but Corky decided that there wasn't – but there was a garden wall, so he just jumped up, walked along the top of it, and dropped down after we had got past.

I don't think any of my Labs would have done that. It really cemented the new partnership – I trusted him enough to let him use his initiative, and when something like that happens, you know you've got the right dog.

Name Shame

Simon Want, vet

Often, rather unusual pet names are given to animals. When combined with the owner's surname, the results can be unfortunate. One gentleman, whose surname was Shufflebottom, had a small terrier called Wobbles.

Pug Groupies

Kay White, author and journalist

I have always thought that, in the evenings, when they lie beside me on the sofa, my Pugs were fast asleep; they surprised me one evening by revealing that they were actually watching television with a great deal of comprehension.

The Crufts programme was on, and suddenly the young male Pug who had won Best of Breed appeared on the screen.

My two Pug girls rushed at the television, whining, muttering and spitting with joy as only Pugs can do. They stood up on their hind legs to reach the dog's face, smothering him with wet Puggy kisses, absolutely entranced with excitement and pleasure.

When he vanished from the screen, they came back to sit down, and were completely uninterested in all the other breeds.

Whatever would they do if they were at a show and

their handsome hero actually appeared in the ring?
Would they dash at him, waving autograph books? And
would he take off his collar and throw it to them? Has
the Pug breed, which is rumoured to have lived as pets
with humans for hundreds of years, begun to copy
human behaviour?

This is the first time I have known dogs to recognise
images on the television screen, but it's a good excuse
for getting a larger model!

Simon The Trainspotter

Angus McKenzie, guide dog owner

Simon, a Golden Retriever, was trained at Redbridge, Essex, in 1989 and was my first guide dog. About four years after he had joined me, I was faced with a journey back from Otford, near Sevenoaks, to King's Cross, and thence to Finchley Central, where I live.

I had been visiting a friend, and had checked with the then British Rail that the service was working normally. The train travels from Sevenoaks, via Otford and Swanley, to Blackfriars, then King's Cross and up to Hertfordshire.

By about 9pm on a Sunday night, we had reached Bromley South, the last station where I could have changed to a Victoria train. Just after leaving the station, another passenger asked me where I was going. I mentioned King's Cross, to be told that there was an announcement that the train was terminating at Blackfriars.

I didn't know Blackfriars, so I elected to change at Elephant and Castle, where I could switch to the underground and go direct to Finchley.

I left the train at Elephant and Castle, to discover, with a degree of horror, that no one else got off. I had never been to Elephant station, so I waited for quite a while to try to get some clues.

We were taught to take a series of deep breaths if there was a panic situation, and then I heard a train passing in the opposite direction on the other side of the platform. This gave me the clue that the platform was an island, so I could give Simon the command "Find the stairs", with a rather dodgy sense of confidence. I didn't want to let Simon see that I was worried.

So, he soon found some stairs, and we went down, eventually reaching a hall with a pronounced echo. I again waited, and eventually another passenger ran past in a hurry, but allowed me a few seconds by pointing my hand in the direction of the exit. He told me to go down to the lights, turn left, down to the next lights, then left again, down the road, where I would eventually find the tube station. He explained that the normal connection tunnel was closed because of vandals.

So, we walked down to the lights, turned left, then again, and then I remembered that I always said to Simon "Find the tube" when we were nearing Finchley Central. I wondered whether he had heard me, but, in a few more steps, he swerved to the left, into a building, and stopped. A voice said that this was Elephant and Castle, with the comment "You are new in these parts, can I help you?", so, he found another passenger to take me down to the northern line, quite late at night.

On an occasion like this, the dog's excellent training really shines through. Guide dogs have much more intelligence than most people realise.

On another occasion, I was on my way to a British Astronomical Association meeting at the Scientific Society, in New Burlington Place, off Saville Row and Regent Street.

I had crossed Regent Street, and walked north to New Burlington Place, whereupon Simon stopped, obviously puzzled. A voice called out: "You can't come down here, as it is covered with hot tarmac."

I calmly said to Simon that we would have to go round the block, little thinking that he would understand. He had never been on the alternative route, but calmly walked down Regent Street. Just as I was prepared to go by the rule book and give him the kerb then right command, he passed in front of me and pulled me round to the right.

He did the same at Saville Row, then once again into the opposite end of New Burlington Place. After a few steps, he pulled me round to the right, up some stone steps, and to the door of the Scientific Society. What more can one ask of a guide dog? Someone had been following me, and had been prepared to help, but he admitted that he was astounded at Simon's actions.

Great Portland Street used to be the station for the old premises of the RNIB. After a meeting, we made our way to the westbound platform, and waited for a metropolitan train. It came in, the doors opened, and I asked Simon to take me into the train.

The doorway was blocked by two people talking, so I had to walk right, to the single door, to get in. I thought I had reached the spot, and went forward, holding out my cane, found the gap, and went ahead. Simon jumped up and pushed me back. I had forgotten that there were no single doors on this type of rolling stock, and I nearly fell between the ends of the coaches. We could only have been inches from the edge.

Another time, I went to a local meeting in Finchley at which Margaret Thatcher was to be present. Needless to say, she eventually came over and knelt down to stroke Simon. He has the distinction of being perhaps the only living thing that has ever made a Prime Minister kneel!

You can imagine that these sort of events make the blind guide dog owner very fond indeed of their dog. It is a very special relationship – not just a working one, but a close friendship.

Once, I was taking a blind BBC classical music producer back to the southbound bus stop in Regent's Park Road, Finchley, and reached an island in the middle of a zebra crossing. The producer had a long cane, and Simon was on my left as usual, waiting for the "Forward" command.

A car stopped in the nearest lane, the outside one, and I gave the command to go. My friend was on my right, and as we passed the front left wheel, Simon gave me the emergency stop movement and caused me to push my friend back, nearly knocking her over. While I quickly retreated, a car, travelling at around 70 kilometres an hour, passed on the inside, missing me by around 30 centimetres – Simon was even closer.

The motorist who had stopped came over, and told me that Simon had saved both of us from being killed by this speeding car. Unfortunately, no one got the registration number.

In 2001, I was walking down the steps to the southbound platform at Finchley Central, and heard someone move. I asked if there was a train in, and was told that there was. I approached the train carefully, holding out the baton, and suddenly Ward, my present dog, leapt up and pushed me back, just as I was about to go over the edge, with a train actually entering the station.

The lady apologised, saying that she didn't speak very good English good. I commented that she had spoken perfect English when I had originally talked to her.

Finally, when I was walking down Hendon Lane (Finchley), I encountered a plank that had been left right across the pavement. For the first time in 43 years of blindness, I fell forwards. Ward tore in front, and hurled his body through 90 degrees, so I would fall on him, breaking my fall. Indeed, I did – when my hands did reach the pavement, the momentum had greatly diminished, as I fell across Ward's back. It was lucky that neither of us were hurt.

So, these are some stories that will explain to the reader what having a guide dog is all about. They seem to have a sixth sense, and will do anything to save their owner, the leader of the pack, from coming to any harm.

The Old Lad Dog

Barbara Swann, Working Collie specialist

Even when he was young, he was always called the Old Lad Dog because of his thick coat and grizzly colouring. He was utterly serious and totally committed to working sheep. I never sent him out to fetch sheep – seen or unseen – but he'd return with his sheep, and never let me down. I always had sheep – though maybe not always the right ones!

On holiday, in a cottage on the top of Exmoor, I got up one morning and went outside to drink in the view, Lad at my side. I never saw him go, or knew where he went, but he'd gone. I was worried that he'd be shot for rounding up sheep, for I knew that's what he was up to. I whistled and called for what seemed forever.

Then I saw a horse come over the top through a gap in the wall, followed by a cow, followed by a flock of sheep, followed by old Lad. Extremely embarrassing!

Later that day, the farmer from below came up to the cottage and asked if I'd sell the dog. He'd watched Old Lad Dog working and thought him to be brilliant!

On another occasion at a trial, I sent him out to unseeable sheep. He ran wide and disappeared, never ending up at the sheep. I called and whistled. No dog. As before, it was an area unknown to us both. I returned from the course, the trial continued, and I tried to find him down the hill in the distance.

I saw him pass through a herd of deer on some scrub land, without disturbing them, and continue out of sight in the far distance to a golf course and beyond. I was out of my mind with worry.

Not knowing what to do, I stood there looking where I had last seen him. Then, in the far distance, I saw a flock of sheep moving across the golf course in a manner sheep only manage with a good dog in command. I whistled my recall command and they advanced across the course until I could fetch them no further because of a stone wall.

I commanded a return and he came, leaving an illegally lifted flock of sheep on the golf course. Poor Old Lad: having missed the sheep he left, he couldn't return to me without sheep – wherever they came from.

So dedicated was Old Lad that, on one occasion, I

asked him to hold a small flock in the corner of a field while I finished a gate repair. Job done, I told the dogs at my feet to get into the jeep and we set off for home (around 20 miles away), stopping for a snack on the way.

Eventually, some two hours later, we arrived home. I opened the jeep back – no Lad! Panic wasn't the word. I drove back like a maniac. Bless him, he was still there doing what I had asked, never doubting I'd be back.

But that was the Old Lad Dog. All the top trial men from *One Man and His Dog* had offered to buy him from me. No money can buy a dog like that, he was priceless. Anyway, he was my friend and teacher.

At one trial, I made a mistake and gave a wrong command. Usually, he'd know I was wrong, ignore me and do the right thing; this day, he didn't. At the end of

my run, I came off the field and a well-known man came and said, "I'll still buy him off you even though he made a mistake."

"He didn't. I gave him the wrong command."

"Thought so," he said, "I've never seen him make a mistake."

Yes, we had some great runs.

Nell was a daughter of old Lad and just as dedicated. My youngest son, Andrew, got quite interested in competing and would run Nell – she always corrected any mistake that was made.

On this occasion, Andrew had a really bad day, getting all his commands wrong. The audience was silent, watching what happened. Nell brought the sheep round the back of him to start the drive, but she then totally ignored him, and, on her own with no commands, took the flock to the pen designated for the sheep that had competed. It was Nell's way of saying to him, "I ain't being messed about by you and your stupid commands," and she put them in, left, and came down. It was talked about in our circle for several years!

The intelligence of the collie! Nell knew she couldn't leave the sheep on the course and that they had to be put away before she came off. And they say dogs can't think for themselves.

Doggie Deception

Murray Simmonds, Sergeant, Ministry of Defence (Police Dogs)

People's initial perceptions of dogs can often be totally wrong. The friendly-looking little Yorkie often turns out to be a damn sight more dangerous than some of the GSDs I have come across, and this story is about such an encounter.

A good friend of mine was leaving the police service and had joined a security company that specialised in overseas engagements. He asked me to locate, purchase and train six GSDs for guard work; so, with the help of a group of friends, I set about the task.

I saw an advertisement in a local trade paper for a 12-month-old GSD called Max. The asking price was reasonable, so I set off with my friend, Steve King, to view the dog.

We approached the Avonmouth Dock area and proceeded down a scruffy lane, which terminated at an even more scruffy car scrapyard. As we approached the gates, I saw the beast from hell hanging off the wire fence in a compound near the owner's caravan. Judging by the state of his coat, he had never seen a comb. The compound contained eight food bowls and more excrement than a small elephant could pass.

The owner approached and we exchanged pleasantries, which basically involved him trying to double the original asking price of the dog. I became somewhat suspicious when his partner refused to leave the caravan whenever the gate to Max's compound was opened.

When I asked why there were so many food bowls in the pen, I was told that he threw one in, and while the dog was eating, he pulled one out with a stick. When asked if the dog was ever taken out for exercise, the owner tried to sell me a Ford Escort. He also told me he wanted rid of him, as he was going to buy two Rottweilers. By this time, I was beginning to despair.

Out of pure pity for this dog, and at the risk of certain mortal injury, I asked the owner to place a leash on him, so I could walk him away from the yard. A grim look was my reply, and, as the gate opened, a loop of twine was thrown over his neck.

Steve, having a strange sense of humour at times, looked on with amusement as I took the string and set off for the gate on to the lane. He hadn't yet bitten me, to my amazement.

Max was viewing Steve and me in a less than friendly manner as we set off down the lane. But for a dog that had never been out of that compound, his behaviour wasn't too bad. I was beginning to get cocky when my deluxe 'lead' gave way and Max took off down the lane.

Being a professional dog handler, I decided to wait 30 seconds before panicking, but, to my amazement, Max came back. I tied a better knot in the twine, walked back, put him in the car, handed over far too much money and away we went.

Once groomed and given some TLC, Max turned into a friendly and biddable dog, who, incidentally, never did go abroad. He spent his days as a companion to one of our officers.

The moral of this story is that initial appearances can be deceptive.

A Diamond In The Ruff

Danni Curtis, guide dog owner

Cynophobia (a fear of dogs) is not normally a good basis for guide dog ownership, but that is what I suffered from as a child. My parents tried everything to help me overcome this fear but to no avail.

At the age of five, I was sent to a boarding school for the blind where my fear soon manifested itself when I came into contact with my music teacher's guide dog, Ruff. As soon as I was aware that the dog was near me, I ran screaming from the room in terror. No amount of reassurance by matron and the other staff would persuade me to go back to the music room until Ruff had been removed from it.

My first year at school passed and still my fear of dogs had not been allayed. One day, I was sitting on a coach on my way to Weston-Super-Mare for our annual school trip to the seaside. Not far from me sat my music teacher and Ruff. I was looking forward with eager anticipation to the day ahead and Ruff was temporarily forgotten.

Recently there had been a slight improvement in my reaction to Ruff, but the fear was still very much in evidence. It seemed to me that Ruff would try to come near me whenever she could, and, when off the lead, she would choose to sit near me over and above the other children in the class. Perhaps she could sense my fear and was trying to help me overcome it?

That day, I was feeling quite relaxed and was chatting animatedly with the other children around me. Suddenly I felt a gentle nudge against my leg. I put my hand down and felt a soft, velvety head. This time I did not recoil – there was nowhere to run in the coach. I tentatively stroked the head and felt quite calm. I was finally overcoming my fear of dogs thanks to that gentle, calm guide dog. I even insisted on sitting near to Ruff on our return journey from Weston!

Twenty years later, I trained with my first guide dog, Alma, and haven't looked back since. I am now a dogaholic and am working with my fourth guide dog, Dixy.

Thanks to Ruff, I have been able to enjoy the independence, companionship and dignity that a guide dog brings, not to mention the numerous friends I've made over the years through being a guide dog owner.

The Millennium Dog

Staff, Canine Partners

The Japanese television crew watched, cameras whirling, as Endal the yellow Labrador leapt up at the cash machine, and, with his mouth, 'handed' the credit card and a wad of £10 notes to his master, 42-year-old Allen Parton. "That's amazing," said producer Masaki Mochizuki from Super Television, one of Japan's national television networks. "What else can he do?"

Endal was keen to show him. Back at Allen's home in Clanfield, Hampshire, he opened the washing machine with his nose, pulled out several pairs of socks, carefully dropping them into the laundry basket, ready to hang on the line. Then, on command, he opened a kitchen cupboard, tugging at a purple cord hanging from the handle, and nosed out a packet of cereal, carrying it in his mouth to Allen in his wheelchair. Finally, he sat on the chair at the kitchen table, while Allen had breakfast, ready to 'hand' his owner anything if he needed it.

Four years earlier, however, when Endal was born, no one thought that this lonely little puppy was particularly special. If anything, he was something of a misfit, since his parents, who were owned by a Southampton breeder, were father and daughter. Not realising that the bitch was still in season, they put her in with her father, only to discover soon afterwards that she was pregnant.

Such pregnancies can fail to develop or can result in sickly or malformed pups. Amazingly, Endal, the only puppy in the litter, seemed perfectly normal. Even so, his owners, Barry and Sue Edwards, did not know what to do with him. Unable to register him because of his parentage, they considered keeping him as a pet until a month later when Canine Partners – a charity that trains dogs to aid the independence of disabled people – visited to inspect another litter.

"I happened to walk into the room and saw this very pretty puppy sitting all on his own," recalls Nina Bondarenko, programme director for Canine Partners. "I said, 'Hello little yellow chap, what's the matter with you?' Then I asked if I could put him through the aptitude tests that we set dogs to see if they would be suitable assistants for people who need help."

These tests are a series of simple exercises to measure each dog's interest in people, co-operation, and flexibility. Nina started by placing Endal on his back to see if he licked rather than struggled. He did the former, which was a sign that he was adaptable and calm. Nina also put Endal in another room, which he didn't know so well, while she hid. The puppy sat and thought for a while and then started to search for her. This was exactly what Nina had been hoping he would do because it suggested he had initiative and wanted to be with people. Nina also gave him a spoon and then called him to her. Instead of hanging on to the spoon, he handed it over – another good sign.

However, he wasn't very enthusiastic. He did some of these things rather half-heartedly, as if he was saying, "Well, I'll do it if you want but it is a bit of a bore." Nina could also tell that he was sensitive and not the bravest dog in the universe; when she held him in the air, his body went rigid and he tucked his tail under. Nina's instinct (which she has learned to rely on during her 30 years' experience) told her that even if Endal wasn't as keen as she hoped, one day he would be right for someone.

So Canine Partners bought him from the breeder, Barry Edwards, and found Judith Turner to act as his puppy parent or 'foster mother'. Judith, who had not long lost her black Labrador, Fennel, to cancer, quickly realised that Endal (named after a local vet) was a one-woman dog. Although he remained aloof during training sessions at the centre, he absolutely adored Judith and would lick her all over every time he saw her – even if she'd only walked out of the room for a few seconds!

"Endal kept me on the straight and narrow after Fennel's death and would do absolutely anything for me," says Judith. "However, there was one big problem – Endal hated us leaving him alone at night and would get upset when we left him in his basket downstairs. Then, by chance, we thought of leaving a nightlight on. From that night on, he slept like a baby – he'd simply been scared of the dark! We also bought him a huge pink teddy bear to cuddle up to."

Endal quickly became adept at jobs such as finding keys and taking off Judith's jacket. But his personality also shone through when he was off-duty. "When I took him to a local village concert, he tried to out-sing the chief tenor by howling above him!" recalls Judith. "He also adored the smell of port. At Christmas, we came downstairs to find he had opened a bottle of port with his teeth – but he'd left it standing upright on the carpet, without having spilt one drop. He had just wanted to sniff it one more time!"

Yet as Endal continued to do his training at the centre, he had something of a half-hearted attitude. Nina couldn't help thinking there was something missing. Somehow, despite his obvious intelligence, the dog lacked dynamism and didn't seem to sparkle. It was as though he was waiting for something – or someone – to happen in life in order to release his full potential.

Endal was the kind of puppy who was choosy about who he bonded with. When, as part of his training, he did a three-week swap with another family to help him adapt to different environments, Endal took a while to adjust. Although he did what he was told, he withdrew into himself. Nina began to realise that she needed to find him a full-time partner whom he could really relate to, just as he had bonded with Judith. If she couldn't find the right person, Endal would never achieve his full potential, and, for an intelligent dog, that seemed a great waste.

There was also another added complication – Endal was showing signs of going lame. "Puppies often do this, on and off, as part of their growing process while their bones knit together," explained Nina. "It's known as panosteitis, like growing pains in children. But it was happening too often to Endal, so we had him X-rayed. The results showed that he might have osteochondritis dessicans, a fault in the elbow joint. Some dogs get better on their own accord but others get worse and have to be operated on, which would mean they wouldn't be able to work. We weren't sure with Endal. So we decided to rest him and see what happened."

Meanwhile, only five miles away, the future was looking bleak for Allen Parton. In 1991, Allen, then a weapons electronics officer in the Royal Navy, had waved goodbye to his wife, Sandra, and their two children, Liam and Zoe, aged six and five, to fight in the Gulf War. As they set off, Allen and his men had been told that 15 per cent of them wouldn't come back. But like many brave servicemen, Allen was certain this wouldn't apply to him. After all, he'd already served in the Falklands and Northern Ireland and had come out unscathed. Why should his luck run out this time?

But it did. Within a month of arriving, Allen's military car was smashed up in a serious accident, which shattered both his body and mind forever. His first memory was waking up in a British hospital six weeks later and thinking, "Where am I?" His right-hand side had lost all feeling and he had only 50 per cent of his memory. The effects were catastrophic. Allen couldn't recognise family or friends, let alone remember the names for items like 'bed'. He only knew Sandra was his wife because the nurses would say, "Your wife is here". Even more terrifying, he couldn't recall getting married or having the children.

In a flash – literally – Allen had gone from a healthy father of two to an angry, wheelchair-bound invalid who couldn't talk properly and whose words spilled out of his mouth in a haphazard, disorderly fashion without making sense.

"The fear and shock made me furious," admits Allen. "I refused to accept I was disabled and I'm ashamed to say that I was horrible and rude to everyone." He was also plunged into a deep, fathomless depression from which there seemed no escape. Twice, he tried to commit suicide. It was, he told himself, the only way out.

Allen spent the next five years in hospital and rehabilitation. When he finally came home, Sandra, who had been forced to give up her job as a nurse to look after her husband, was at her wits' end. Then she saw an article about Canine Partners in a local newspaper. Desperate to do something for herself, as well as looking after Allen, she became a puppy-walker to Ferdy, a yellow Labrador. The distraction and light relief provided by a lively puppy in the house helped the whole family – even though Allen still found it difficult to talk and communicate.

One day, in the summer of 1997, Allen's usual bus for his day centre failed to turn up. Sandra told him in no uncertain terms that she wasn't prepared to have him moping around the house. He would have to go to the Canine Partners centre with her. Although he didn't see it then, Fate had just stepped in. Allen's life was about to change dramatically once more.

But as he sat in the training centre that morning, in his wheelchair parked in the corner of the room, refusing to speak or join in, Allen didn't realise this. Instead, he would rebuff anyone who tried to ask him a question, by telling them to talk to his wife. He felt horribly self-conscious and it was easy to see why. Not only was he unable to speak clearly but his body was continually twitching. He refused to make eye contact with anyone and was very self-conscious and uncomfortable.

Not far away from his chair sat a group of puppies, resting in between training sessions. One of them, happened to be Endal. "He started looking at Allen and, as he did so, Allen glanced back," said Nina, who constantly observes the dogs to consider which applicants they might suit. "Endal then looked up again and seemed to say, 'Mmm, I quite like you', and then Allen put his hand down to give him a pat. Immediately, Endal leapt up on Allen's lap and gave a big, slobbery grin. Allen smiled as if to say, 'This dog really likes me!' Then, almost without knowing why he was doing it, Allen began to rub Endal under his jacket. It so happens that Endal loves being rubbed at exactly that spot. He looked up at Allen as if to say 'You are my man!'"

It was nothing short of a miracle, a dramatic turning point that both Allen and Endal had needed so badly in their lives.

As Allen left the centre that day, there was a certain sparkle in his eyes, which hadn't been there for a very long time. He could hardly wait until the next week when Endal was coming back to the centre with his puppy-walker. Allen made sure that he was there too, and, over the next few weeks, Endal made a beeline for him as soon as he came in through the door. The two would sit next to each other and Endal would reach out and touch him with his paw. As Nina points out, until he met Allen, Endal hadn't been anything special. It was the combination of his character with Allen's that made the winning ticket. Two parts really are greater than the whole.

Just as Endal had helped Judith through her bereavement, so it seemed that Endal wanted to now help Allen. Even so, it wouldn't have been right for Nina to have suggested that Allen and Endal were partnered immediately. She had to wait until Allen applied for a dog himself.

It took nearly five months for the assessment procedures and paperwork to go through. "I had to fill in a form, describing my disabilities, and this was the first time I had admitted there was something wrong with me," recalls Allen. "It was a cathartic experience, which finally gave me the hope I needed.

"Until I met Endal, I was in the depths of despair. But when he refused to leave my side in that training centre, I suddenly saw a chink of light. Endal had found me and wasn't willing to let me go. He was living proof that angels don't just come on two legs."

But before Allen could take Endal home, he had to go through an intensive two-week residential training course. During that time, Nina noticed a dramatic change in Endal's behaviour. "Instead of doing jobs half-heartedly, he'd leap to it! 'Keys,' he'd say, 'you want me to get keys? Great. Hang on and I'll run and get them.' Before, when someone else was asking him to do it, he'd amble over to the keys and back again without any great incentive. In return, he seemed to understand how much Allen had been through. He's an interesting combination of pushiness and sensitivity."

Endal's most amazing skill is his ability to use his
initiative and read situations quickly. This was exactly
what Allen needed to help him cope with his severe
injuries. Would Endal be able to help? They would soon
find out when he joined the Parton household full-time
in autumn 1997.

Still unable to speak properly, Allen also suffered from
word blindness when he simply couldn't find the words
to give Endal a command. "One morning, I realised I'd
left my razor upstairs. I could see a picture of the razor
in my head but couldn't think of the word. So I just
patted my cheeks in an attempt to understand. To my
amazement, Endal ran up the stairs and came down with
the razor in its leather case."

Over the ensuing months, Allen and Endal began to
create their own sign language. A pat on the head means
that Allen wants his cap. Instantly, Endal darts round to
the back of the wheelchair where the cap is inside Allen's
bag. Hands held up mean gloves are required, and Endal
finds them and brings them round the front to Allen.

Allen and Endal began to be photographed by local
newspapers, and then, as they grew in confidence, they
were nominated for an award in a national competition
run by *Dogs Today* magazine. During one photographic
session, Endal and Allen went shopping to show how
Endal could differentiate between tins and bottles, and
nose out whatever Allen asks for on the shelves. As they
were leaving, Allen realised he needed money from the
cash machine outside. With the sunlight shining on the
glass screen, making it difficult for Allen to see, and with
the money and receipt slot set far up the back of the
machine, Allen was struggling. Suddenly, without being
asked, Endal jumped up to retrieve the card and money
when Allen had made his transaction.

Newspaper photographers asked him to do it again
and again so they could get their pictures. This was the

photograph that was used when Endal was voted Dog of the Millennium in the *Dogs Today* competition. Soon, Endal was splashed over nearly every front page. The press went wild and reporters from around the world wanted to know about this extraordinary dog. He was filmed by crews almost daily. People started to recognise the yellow Labrador as "Endal the cashpoint dog."

But the most amazing example of Endal's initiative happened in May 2001 when he and Allen were invited to a stand at Crufts. After checking into a hotel the night before, Allen took Endal outside for a run across a green on the other side of the hotel car park. As usual, his lead was clipped to the chair. Suddenly, a car reversed towards them at 40mph. Endal was between Allen and the car, so, instinctively, he pushed the dog out of the way. Seconds later, the car knocked the chair over and Allen blacked out.

When he came round, Allen found Endal pulling his body over, using his teeth on his jacket, to put Allen into the recovery position. The dog then ran back for Allen's mobile phone, which he got out of the bag and thrust against his face. After that, he went back for his blanket from the chair and then ran up to the hotel reception, barking for help.

The story hit the national headlines. Endal, it appeared, was the first dog who had ever put a human into the recovery position, without being taught. Once again, he was a familiar face on the television and in the news. Everyone wanted footage of this remarkable dog. But fame came at a price. Endal had over-stretched himself by jumping up at the cashpoint so many times, and the following day, he went severely lame during a fund-raising event.

Allen's world was crashing down around him once again. A lame dog would be unable to fulfil his work properly and could even be taken off the Canine Partners programme to be rehomed as a pet. Allen and Endal were in severe danger of losing each other unless they could do something about it.

Allen and Sandra visited several vets, all of whom agreed that strict rest was needed. However, this was difficult, as Endal refused to leave Allen's side. When Allen left the room, so did Endal. Going upstairs exacerbated the lameness; Allen had always refused a stairlift, preferring to be independent. So the only option was to shut Endal in the kitchen at night in an attempt to make him rest.

In the morning, however, the Partons found that Endal had jumped up on the kitchen work surface and had eaten one kilogram of rabbit food from its bag. "It was as though he was doing it to attract attention and say 'How dare you shut me out?'" said Allen.

He also had the swing bin lid round his neck, which could have been dangerous. There was only one solution to ensure strict bed rest – kennels. Allen, in floods of tears, was unable to take Endal himself, so Alison, one of the trainers at Canine Partners, volunteered.

For two weeks, Endal had to stay in a very small cage, which limited his movement. He had one short break and that was to the vet. Meanwhile, Allen admitted that he was acting like a bear with a sore head. "I was angry with everyone and behaved like a child. By the end of two weeks, Endal was still limping. The vet said that he might get better but he might not."

Endal came back for the afternoon but Allen confessed that he was unable to cope with the uncertainty. "If he came home and then had to go again, because of his health problems, it would have destroyed me." So Heather, Canine Partners' training manager, took Endal to her home for the night and put him back in kennels the following morning.

However, neither had reckoned on Endal's determination not to give up – or Sandra's. Furious with her husband, she told him to stop being so selfish and to think of someone else instead of himself – that "person", of course, was Endal. She told Allen, in no uncertain words, that the dog needed him badly at this moment in his life but that Allen wasn't there for him.

It was the best thing she could have said. Unable to drive himself, because of his disability, Allen leapt into action. He asked Alison to collect Endal from the kennels and to bring him home, where he belonged. Even if he ended up limping for the rest of his life, Allen pledged to himself that he would be there to take away the dog's hurt and pain, just as Endal would do for him.

Endal came home, his tail wagging energetically with excitement. He and Allen were now a 'marriage', for better or for worse.

During the next few months, Endal was put on a strict diet of additive-free meat and cereal to help his arthritis along with a gentle exercise regime and a quiet period to heal. Slowly, he has continued to improve, and, although Endal has bad days – just as Allen has – the arthritis appears to be under control.

Meanwhile, miraculously, Allen's speech was improving dramatically and his twitching had almost stopped. Indeed, to hear him now, it's hard to believe that it was almost incomprehensible, despite five years of speech therapy. Neither Allen nor Sandra are certain how Endal achieved this, although Allen thinks it was because he desperately wanted to talk back to a dog who obviously loved him so much.

Even more touching, Endal talks too. A dog normally only has eight different voice patterns, but Endal has 20. According to the tone, they mean all kinds of things, ranging from 'I love you' to 'Can't we switch television channels?' (his favourite programmes are those with animals in them).

Allen lifts Endal on to his knee to tickle his huge tummy and demonstrate how he 'talks'. Endal looks up at his master adoringly and howls with pleasure. The noise is so loud that I half expect someone to knock on Allen's front door to see what's going on. In fact, the neighbours are used to it.

Allen and his dog are well known in Clanfield. Because of his poor memory, which means Allen can usually only remember things for 48 hours, he also forgets people's names and faces. Before Endal came into his life, Allen was too embarrassed to go out much or talk to friends who could remember him even though he had no idea who they were. "Now, they come up to talk about Endal and even if I don't know who they are, Endal provides a talking point. They stroke and chat to him, which helps me to socialise again."

Endal has also helped Allen's marriage and the relationship with his children, Liam, now 16, and Zoe, 15. "They all love him even though Endal very obviously prefers me! He sleeps on my side of the bed, touching my wheelchair with his paw. And when Sandra and I sit on the sofa, watching television, he jumps up between us."

Sandra, an amazing woman who has put up with more than most wives would cope with, accepts this. "Life will never be the same again, but, thanks to Endal, Allen has a second chance – and so do we. Out of 80 seriously injured married men in the Gulf War, only eight marriages survived. Ours is one of them. The children lost their old dad but now Endal has given them a new one."

Allen and Endal's daily routine illustrates this. Endal wakes Allen every morning, without fail, at 7am – even when he wants a lie-in. Sometimes Allen tries to keep his eyes closed, pretending he's asleep, but one small gesture to signify otherwise, and Endal is on the bed! He pulls the wheelchair towards Allen's side, using the purple cord that hangs from the back for this purpose. Everything that needs opening in the Parton household has a 'tug' on it like this; purple is Endal's favourite colour.

Endal will then put up the loo seat for Allen, using his nose, and, like a typical male, fails to put it down again after use! He then helps Allen dress, by opening his underwear drawer and pulling out clean socks and pants. Although there are obvious limits on how far Endal can 'dress' Allen, he can master handing him clothes and can even manage zips on cardigans.

Following Endal downstairs on his bottom, Allen will say "Cereal" and Endal will open a floor-level cupboard and nose out a packet of cereal, which he hands to his master in the chair.

During the morning, Allen will either go with Sandra to the Canine Partners' centre to talk to other possible dog recipients, or he'll answer Endal's emails, which average 50 to 100 every day, often as a spin-off from Endal's own website. Together, they also manage basic household tasks, such as tidying up the sitting room, turning off lights, collecting the post, and putting food back in the cupboard.

Towards lunch, the couple often amble down to the shop where Endal and Allen are a familiar sight. "Soup!" commands Allen, and Endal will nose out a tin of tomato flavour (one of Allen's favourites) to hand to his master. Sometimes, as a treat, Allen will ask Endal to pick a lucky dip scratch-card. So far he's won £40.

While crossing the road, Endal will sit firmly on the pavement if a car is coming, to prevent his master from crossing. Allen's short-term memory means that he can forget to look, and the first time that Endal refused to budge, Allen thought he was being difficult. Then he realised. Endal was trying to warn him that a car had just come round the roundabout.

At the chemist, Allen will often wait outside in his chair while Endal goes in, wallet in his mouth, to collect Allen's prescription. In fact, Endal is Allen's best medicine, as shown when passers-by pause to admire his beautiful golden coat and permanent grin. "He breaks the ice," explains Allen. "Before he came into my life, I wouldn't talk to people. But I'd have to be pretty miserable to ignore someone who likes my dog."

Back for lunch and Endal will hand Allen a plate of sandwiches, which Sandra has made him earlier. In the afternoon, it's off to the park to play or perhaps to catch up on a bit of television. If one of Allen's legs happens to slip out of his chair, Endal will gently pick up the trouser hem in his mouth and put it back.

At least once a week, if not more, Allen and Endal will make guest appearances on television or at charity events. During the last 18 months, Endal – ever the willing performer – has entertained 98 film crews! Endal has also won a string of awards, including Dog of the Millennium, Golden Bonio Dog of the Year, Assistance Dog of the Year 2001 and Pro-dog Dog of the Year Gold Medal. He has been on television all over the world, from the United States and Canada to Japan and Australia.

But besides relishing the spotlight, Endal has a kind heart and an uncanny knack for spotting those who need special help. He is particularly good at bringing autistic children out of themselves, and during a recent trip made a little boy smile for the very first time.

Just as miraculous, Endal met a five-year-old girl with cerebral palsy. Allen, scared that Endal might knock her over with an over-enthusiastic lick, asked her to sit up straight in her wheelchair instead of leaning to one side. "She can't do that on her own," said her mother – and then stopped in amazement. Her daughter, desperate to see this 'miracle dog', had managed to ease herself into an upright position so she could cradle Endal in her arms. There wasn't a dry eye in the room.

Allen also visits injured men and women who are still coming to terms with their disabilities. One of his toughest watersheds was to go back to RAF Headly Court, the Epsom-based military rehabilitation centre where Allen had suffered the dark depths of despair after his accident. "I couldn't have walked through those doors without Endal, but when we did, it was as though I had exorcised all my demons," he says.

There, Allen and Endal met a young man who was paralysed from his head downwards after jumping into a swimming pool. "That was me, ten years ago," said Allen. "So I told him about Endal and the joy he had brought me. Hopefully, that man will find his own Endal in life."

No one, however, could be exactly like Endal. Not only is he intelligent and perceptive but he also has character. Take his daily walk to the shops when, after being released from the lead to sniff the local green, he simply had to dash off to sniff a cat. Then there was last Christmas, when he simply couldn't resist helping himself to a few turkey titbits by opening the fridge door.

Weekly weighing sessions, however, ensure that Endal is not allowed too many illicit snacks. If he's a jot over his average weight of 31 kilograms, it's smaller portions to make sure that he's fit enough to do his job. Thankfully, Endal's arthritis seems to be going through a good patch, although he continues to have regular six-month check-ups at the vet.

Endal hates to be parted from his master. When Allen and Sandra took a skiing holiday recently, Endal had to go to kennels. As Allen picked him up, he gave him a muted lick, but as soon as they got home and closed the front door, Endal leapt up at him with slobbery kisses. "Men like us dislike public shows of affection!" jokes Allen.

But what about the future? "Most Canine Partners' dogs retire after about ten years, but I'm going to ask if I can keep him," says Allen firmly. "I couldn't imagine another dog. After all, he's my be all and *end all*."

Prickly Situation

Jenny Moir, head of PR, Hearing Dogs for Deaf People

Esko, a Shetland Sheepdog, woke his recipient, Edna, one night, and she thought he was alerting her to the alarm clock. When she checked, she found the alarm had not sounded. She thought Esko was being over-

THANKS PAL!

zealous and went back to sleep.

However, Esko kept alerting her until she thought she had better get out of bed and see what the problem was. He led her to the front door, so she put his lead on and went out into the garden, whereupon he pulled her straight to the kitchen drain, which had been left uncovered by some workmen.

On closer investigation of the drain, Edna found that a tiny hedgehog had got its head jammed between two pipes and its body was dangling down the drain. Esko had heard its high-pitched squealing and realised that something was wrong!

Normandy Landings

Trevor Ireland is a guide dog owner and a former Royal Marine. He was one of the first to go ashore in the 1944 D-Day landings. In an attack on a German gun emplacement he was severely wounded by a mortar explosion, which led to him eventually losing his eyesight.

I have had several guide dogs but Aden, a beautiful German Shepherd, was very special. It was the saddest day of my life when he had to be put down, but he will be remembered by so many people, not least for being the first dog to travel to France and back without undergoing quarantine.

Having regularly travelled to Normandy with my wife, Kate, and fellow surviving members of my regiment, I was determined that Aden should accompany me. To put him through six months' quarantine clearly wasn't acceptable. And so the fight began to change the law. The fight was a long one; it took five years but eventually we got dispensation from the House of Lords.

Finally, on the 3rd February 2000, Lee Stanway (from Bolton Guide Dogs Centre), Kate, Aden and I arrived in Portsmouth, where Aden's documentation was checked thoroughly. Once in France, we met the local vet, who became the first of many French people to admire Aden's good looks and excellent behaviour. Fortunately the vet spoke very good English and the formalities were quickly over.

Aden guided me on the beach where I lost my sight all those years ago; Kate was crying but Aden was steady as a rock. We also laid memorial wreaths during the trip and, at each monument, Aden "sat" to attention. He seemed to know just how to behave in every situation.

On our return to Portsmouth, Aden and I were asked to remain on the ferry until last. Not for any formalities but because the staff all wanted to make a big fuss of Aden! Imagine our added delight when we stepped off the ferry to a surprise fanfare welcome by the Royal Marine soldiers and buglers!

Having travelled by ferry, our next challenge was to take a plane, as I had been invited to a wreath laying ceremony at The Hague. Again, Aden and I faced opposition, with most airlines only allowing dogs to travel in the hold. I rely heavily on my guide dog and, having finally got permission for Aden to travel without quarantine, I was determined that he should stay with me. Finally, common sense prevailed and one airline relented. It's amazing how small Aden managed to make himself so that he could sit neatly at my feet! Again, at the end of the flight, I was asked to remain on board, purely so that all of the crew could stroke him!

Wherever I travelled with Aden, he was the centre of attention – on my frequent visits to hospital I became known by his name rather than my own! A few nurses tried to throw him out but usually he stayed with me on the ward, loved by all. He even played a part in a lady's recovery from an operation by giving her that same attention.

I am so proud of Aden; he was a fantastic companion and a great ambassador for dogs and guide dogs everywhere.

Pregnant Paws

Robert Killick, canine author, columnist and legend!

For the first 25 years of my working life, I was a theatrical person, touring the length and breadth of the country with various shows, plays, musicals, anything. Of course, it was not always convenient to take a dog. However, Jo, who was later to become my wife, had a tiny 5lb Toy Poodle, which she refused to leave behind. The dog was so small, we would pop her into a shopping bag and there she would settle, staying out of sight.

Being members of Equity (the actors' union), we had free entrance into most cinemas for afternoon showings. We often took advantage of this offer, as we had a couple of afternoons a week free.

There was a cinema locally showing a film based in Alaska, which we wanted to see. Unfortunately, we had nowhere to put the dog. It was a bitterly cold day and Jo was wearing a thick, fake-fur coat, so I suggested she stuffed the dog up the front of it, making her look pregnant. In fact, she looked imminent and everyone fussed around her, ushering us past the 'No Dogs' signs and giving us a double seat at the back, near an exit (they may have been thinking she might give birth in their theatre!).

Twenty minutes into the film, a pack of wolves appeared on the screen. The leader threw his head into the air and began to howl. In a trice, the rest of the pack joined in... and so did our Poodle. The exit doors burst open and in stalked four usherettes, shining torches along the rows of seats. The boss girl spoke to me.

"Have you seen a dog?" she asked.

"Yes!" I answered, "On the screen."

"They're wolves, you fool!" she said ungraciously and left.

We settled down for half an hour when the hero dog, seeking his lost mate, howled in his loneliness. Our Poodle, recognising the agony and frustration of the dog, wriggled out from under the coat and howled her answer – "I'm here, come and get me, woohooo!"

Once again, the entrance of the usherettes. Jo was busy stuffing the Poodle out of sight as the torch's beam struck me. I stood up, masking Jo's activities. I said in a loud voice, "I heard it this time! Disgusting I call it, spoiling the enjoyment of the film! Hope you find the swine."

"Thank you, sir," she said, "just doing my job."

We saw the rest of the film in relative peace, and, as we were leaving, the ingratiating manager slid out from under a stone, apologising.

"I hope the disturbance didn't mar your enjoyment of the film, sir."

"No, no," I said, "we find irresponsible oafs wherever we go!"

As I spoke, a strange look came over his face. I followed his gaze. Jo was standing just behind me to one side, and sticking out of the space between two buttons in the middle of the pregnant bump was the Poodle's head, black eyes gleaming.

"It's a miracle!" I exclaimed, "Call me a taxi!" and left hurriedly.

Mutual Trust

Helen McCain, head trainer, Dogs for the Disabled

During my time as a trainer for Guide Dogs for the Blind, I will always remember the first time I tested the understanding of the guiding principle by taking one of the dogs into town, putting a blindfold on, and asking him to take me through town.

With blindfold on, eyes shut, I started off, hesitantly, but then felt my trust and confidence in my dog grew. We flew through town, giving me such a feeling of exhilaration and teaching me a valuable lesson in the importance of trust between man and dog.

A Sweet Tooth

Howard Jones, animal behaviourist and Guide Dogs trainer

Having a job with a difference is always useful as a conversation starter over dinner and indeed has an element of entertainment value factored in for good measure. The nature of a behaviourist's work is both serious and demanding. Telephone calls from anxious or distressed owners at any time of day and night are commonplace. However, seeing the lighter side of animal antics can bring about light relief from the serious cases.

"What is the funniest case you have seen?" is a common after-dinner question, and, without hesitation, the over-amorous Airedale, the fussy feline, or the dog that chased parked cars are overshadowed by the crockery-smashing Boxer.

A young lady telephoned me, saying her dog had smashed three dinner services over three weeks when he was left alone in the house. To capture the evidence, cameras were placed in the lady's home, and, true as her word, the accused Boxer was caught red-handed.

Having climbed on to the work surface, he proceeded to pick up and then toss each piece of crockery from the draining board. As it smashed to the floor he showed not an ounce of remorse, and then the cause of this puzzling behaviour was observed. The crockery was a

mere obstruction between the dog and his reward of sugar cubes, stolen from the container on a shelf above the drainer, each removed with precision to be envied by the most accomplished of thieves.

Once his daily fix had been achieved, this terror-creating Boxer became little more than any other playful canine – and all for what was just a sweet tooth.

There is, of course, a serious side to an animal behaviourist's work. It is the job of a behaviourist to source the cause of a problem and to apply appropriate remedies. Many animals can end up in rescue shelters or rehoming centres through a lack of understanding of their needs. With a little assistance from a professional source, many such cases could be avoided. We spend so much time trying to get our pets to understand us, wouldn't it be better if we spent a little time getting to know them?

Strange Bedfellows

Colin Plum, dog trainer and volunteer at Guide Dogs

I did a home-visit to a lady whose tiny terrier kept attacking her husband. The lady was pleased to see me – as was her husband.

We went up the stairs to a beautiful, large bedroom, where there was a four-poster bed, and, lo and behold, a dog who looked something like a West Highland Terrier. He was puzzled to see this stranger in his bedroom.

Apparently, the usual routine was that the husband came home for lunch, and, with the husband back at work, the lady of the house had a little rest on the bed and took the dog in with her. The dog, therefore, wouldn't tolerate the husband approaching his wife in the bedroom.

It was not too difficult to solve. A few changes for both, especially the wife, in how to treat the dog as a dog and not as a human. She gave him a sanctuary with a cosy dog bed and lots of toys.

I had a nice letter from the owners, saying that all was well and that they were so pleased with the dog that they returned to the original kennels and came back with another pup, this time a neutered bitch. They invited me to see the dogs, which I did, and I got an enthusiastic greeting from both of them.

The owners asked me if I could guess which was the original. I cheated and rolled them both over, amongst much laughter by all concerned.

Bold As Brass

Neil Ewart, Guide Dogs' staff member

Fundraising for any cause often requires a lot of ingenuity and effort. For many years, Guide Dogs has benefited from donations made by the Annual Birmingham International Jazz Festival. The organisers like to name a guide dog after one of the visiting musicians. Early in this collaboration, it was decided to acknowledge the festival's patron, Humphrey Lyttleton.

A photo call was set up, which was to occur during a break in the music. I decided to take a lovely, long-coated German Shepherd Dog, and duly set off.

While the Lyttleton Band was playing, I met up with a reporter and photographer from one of the larger Birmingham newspapers. They wanted a shot of Humph sat on a low wall, pretending to play his trumpet, with the dog sat facing him. "Just like the famous HMV record label."

The time arrived, Humph duly posed, and the dog was placed in position. However, things started to get a bit difficult when the dog saw his reflection in the highly polished instrument. He decided that no way was he going to look in it again and swung his head from left to right. Inspiration eventually struck and the desired photo was obtained.

On stage, at the start of the second session, Humph announced in true *I'm Sorry I Haven't A Clue* double entendre: "The things I do for publicity... I've just shoved a sausage roll up my trumpet!"

Off The Rails

The late Derek Freeman, MBE, former breeding manager at Guide Dogs

Dogs offered to Guide Dogs by the public still often arrived by rail well into the 1960s, even though our own puppy walking scheme was established by then. One day, there was an urgent message asking for someone to go to Leamington Spa station to collect a German Shepherd bitch, as railway staff couldn't get her off the train. When I arrived, the train was still standing in the station but was badly overdue for its departure to Birmingham. The driver was insisting that he had to go!

I flew up the steps, passing a rail staff member who was having his hand dressed – a victim of the German Shepherd!

I got to the guard's van to find four station employees standing by the door peeping into the interior. The poor bitch was going berserk.

One of the staff said, "Be careful, she has just bitten one of our lads, who tried to get her off with a piece of sacking." If you want to torment a dog, wave a piece of sacking, and this, of course, is what had happened.

It now appeared as though they all wanted to witness me being the next victim, and I was surrounded by a rapt audience as I stepped into the van. In fact, their presence only served to aggravate the poor animal. I asked them to go away, and shut the door behind them.

The bitch was on a chain and the mandatory muzzle was tied to the rail behind her. To me, this seemed to be a plan cunningly devised by British Railway (as they were then called) to make the job as difficult as possible.

Eventually, after a lot of threatening behaviour, snapping and flashing of teeth, I managed to get hold of the chain and continued to reassure the bitch. I was just starting to build up some rapport when, suddenly, the van door was flung open. I was just standing up and the bitch caught me a nice one on the elbow, tearing through my jacket and shirt through to the skin.

Understandably, she was badly startled and I had to start all over again. Eventually, I won her confidence sufficiently to get her out of the van, and the train departed. I often wondered what explanation was given on its belated arrival in Birmingham.

The next problem was to get her into my van. On the way out of the station, I remembered that I had already got two dogs in it – a German Shepherd, and, interestingly, a Standard Poodle. Unfortunately, the Poodle had managed to get through the cage at the back and was sitting contentedly on the front seat. The GSD was my own bitch. She was sitting obediently in the back, wagging her tail as I approached with the stranger.

I decided to enlist the help of one of the braver station staff members, who courageously said he was willing to open the back of the van for me. However, he changed his mind when he saw my bitch sitting there: he had just witnessed what a GSD could do!

"No way, mate, you're on your own," he said. And who could blame him?

I was therefore faced with trying to bundle a frightened and aggressive animal in with my extrovert bitch, who was waiting to bounce all over us.

Fortunately, my GSD opted to jump out, and, without any hesitation, the other bitch spotted a sanctuary and leapt into the back.

Experiences like this were not uncommon in the formative years. Incidentally, I drove back with my GSD and the Poodle sat beside me on the passenger seat. The least said about that, the better!

Hat Trick

Kay White, author and journalist

We once had a Boxer bitch named Pixie, who developed a greeting ritual for visitors by carrying a feeding bowl to them. This routine enchanted callers and it never varied... except that once it did!

Our bank manager called in; this was a long time ago, when we were in awe of bank managers. Pixie did her greeting performance to reasonable applause and then our guest was taken round the kennels.

Just as he was leaving after the tour, Pixie arrived, looking very mischievous and carrying in her wet, slobbery mouth a rather battered trilby hat.

"What a shame," the bank manager said, "Pixie has

ruined your husband's hat."

It then fell to me to explain that my husband didn't have a trilby. "I'm so sorry, it must be your hat!" I whimpered.

Suddenly naughty Boxer bitches were not so funny… and he did not buy a puppy!

Hare Of The Dog

Stephen Wright, former Guide Dogs' trainer

Emma was a tiny Whippet, but she was no slouch. If you picture the typical specimen of the breed, with tucked-up tummy and shivering muscles, you obviously never met Emma. She was bred to race, but resembled a small tank. Emma had muscles in places where other Whippets didn't have places..

This was no disadvantage on the track. In fact, those prodigious muscles gave her early pace, which left the majority of her rivals gasping in her slipstream. After a couple of hundred yards, she would burn out, and, at any longer distances, she would find her pursuers floating past as she plugged on, one-paced.

Whippet races are usually staged on a short, straight track. The distance rarely exceeds 175 yards. Emma was a star. Unfortunately, my vanity was less easily satisfied. Sometimes Whippets were raced on Greyhound tracks over 300 yards. Could Emma enhance her reputation, and, by association, mine, by winning over this extended distance? Zealously, I increased her roadwork and built up her stamina. Schooling was achieved at the local track after the electric hare. Emma loved it and ran with all her usual enthusiasm.

At the races, it was a different matter. She still ran well, but the others ran better. In truth, she was being set a task that was not suited to her muscle-bound physique. But I was not satisfied. I was convinced that Emma's failure was due to the fact that the hare had a nasty habit of disappearing at the end of each race, whereas on the short sprints at which she excelled, she would always have the gratifying opportunity of tearing the lure to shreds. Perhaps her lack of success was due to lack of commitment.

Now, it happened that, each week, we would travel to

a Greyhound track in Staffordshire, where an evening of Whippet races would be staged. Emma ran dutifully but without success. After each failure, I would repair to the well-stocked bar in the clubhouse, behind which was probably the worse-stuffed hare in the world. It sat in its glass case in a posture that suggested it had died of some particularly debilitating affliction of the joints. This malady had not only caused the creature great pain, but had also distorted it until it resembled some kind of ghastly hybrid between hare and giraffe. Gazing at it, in my depressed state, inspiration struck.

The next week, just before Emma's race, I resorted to my master plan. Going to the bar, I lifted her up and made a hissing, encouraging noise designed to gee her up. To say it was a success would be an understatement. In the veiled recesses of Emma's pedigree were pit-fighting dogs (perhaps that's where her muscles came from). At the sight of the hare a sound emerged from her throat, which few of us are ever likely to hear. "Is it

a good screamer?" would be a question the old fighting men asked – the strangled shriek of pent-up fury being a much better indication of courage than the frenzied yap of a terrier.

Well, Emma screamed. Conversation in the bar stopped dead. Everyone looked around to see what cruelty might have been inflicted. Aware of the looks, I tried to settle my enraged dog. Eventually, she quietened down. With great embarrassment, I shuffled out of the bar and made my way to the traps.

Unusually, Emma continued to bounce around like a demented demon. Instead of trotting beside me, she continually leapt up at my side, biting my arm, my backside and tearing my jacket to pieces. In passing, I shouted to my wife, "Put the housekeeping on the bitch – she's gone mad!" Dutifully, she set off to the open arms of the bookies.

When you race a Whippet, the whole thing, even on a Greyhound track, lasts for a very short time. If it is your own animal running, then time becomes suspended and you see the whole 20-second race in slow motion.

As the electric hare began out of its gradual acceleration, I watched with bated breath. The traps flew open and Emma hurtled out, kicking back sand in the face of her rivals.

Each stride drove her further ahead. Her muscles bunched and stretched as she ate up the ground. Approaching the bend, she was clearly in front, but this was usual.

As the hare dipped around the bend, she leant over and hurtled behind it. "Now," I thought, "this is where the others start to pull her in; this is where their greater scope pays off, once they have built up to a cruising speed."

The gap remained. The field was making no impression. Emma continued to drive forward as I had never seen her run before. Coming out of the bend, the pursuing pack had still made no impression on her lead.

With barely 50 yards to run, they were clearly outclassed, and I knew that the race was won.

A great breath escaped me, as I realised I had been holding it since the traps opened. "You beauty!" I shouted, but Emma didn't hear me. As she drew level with the clubhouse, she veered sharply away from the rail, to which she had hitherto appeared glued. She crossed the track, ducked under the outer rail and disappeared into the bar.

By the time the other owners had collected their dogs, and the winner had been announced, I had made my way to the bar. A banshee wail, repeated endlessly, led me to my dog.

Amid a sea of bottles, scattered from the shelves in her efforts to reach the hare, was Emma. Froth came from her mouth and her eyes bulged. Even after her lead had been put on and we had driven home, she continued to dance about in a paroxysm of glee.

I was never able to race her on a Greyhound track again. She knew that hares lived behind the bar at each and every one of them – and to hell with the boring, electric imitation!

Tiny Tot

Jenny Moir, head of PR, Hearing Dogs for Deaf People

Tot's recipient, Julia, was asleep one night in the living room while her husband, who had just come out of hospital, was in another room recuperating.

During the night, Yorkshire Terrier Tot went to find Julia and scrabbled at her to wake her up. He then led her to the bathroom where Julia's husband had collapsed and was unconscious on the floor. An ambulance was called and he was rushed to hospital, where he stayed for several months. Julia had heard nothing at all, and if it hadn't been for Tot, Julia is convinced that her husband would have died.

Pass The Parcel

Maurice Hall, former Guide Dogs' trainer

Central Park, New York City. An extremely able and intelligent woman and her guide dog had just removed what happens naturally and put it into a specially designed bag, which was then placed in an outer pouch. In New York, all such equipment looks very up-market and pleasing to the eye!

They proceeded on their journey through the park,

but were interrupted by a young man on a bicycle, who demanded, with menace, the very smart-looking pouch.

Having been reassured that neither her guide dog nor herself would be harmed, she promptly handed over the pouch and its contents. She was instructed by the young man to, "Have a nice day!"

The sun was shining and it was a lovely day in Central Park! Both the owner and the dog continued on their way, feeling that finally the young man had got his 'just deserts'.

Self-confessed Dogaholic

Colin Plum, dog trainer and volunteer at Guide Dogs

I have always been a 'dogaholic' right from my young days. My grandparents had an Airedale called Colonel, and I always went to their house for tea after school. Colonel and I were firm friends. He would get under the table, where I'd secretly feed him titbits from my plate.

Colonel lived for several years and, of course, I was devastated when he died. He was a gentle giant, and, from then onwards, I wanted a dog for myself. But my mother had different ideas.

Time marched on, and I went to Westminster College. In that period, I found that I had an uncle called Mr Hester, who was a guide dog owner with a black Labrador called Rover.

Of course, I had no idea what Guide Dogs was at that time, but when my uncle had to retire Rover in the late-1940s, he got a new dog, and was allowed to rehome Rover to my mother – much to my glee.

I became a sergeant in the Army during my National Service and was stationed at Aldershot. As it wasn't too

far from north London, I used a motorcycle to get
home on some weekends. My mother decided that, if I
was a sergeant, she would be a Lance Corporal in charge
of the dog! Quite often, she went off shopping with
Rover – exercise for him and for herself. It was exercise
for certain – there were a lot of young men in khaki
uniform, who, like me, came home in battledress.
Unfortunately, Rover thought that anybody in khaki was
me, and would keep taking off at high speed. My

I LOVE A MAN
IN UNIFORM!

mother had to apologise many times to petrified
soldiers.

When I came home on leave, there was the usual cup
of tea and home-cooked meal waiting for me. My
mother confessed some time later that Rover always got
excited about 15 to 20 minutes before I arrived, so she
was always prepared. As for the motorbike, I had to add
a sidecar because Rover wanted to go where I went.
How daft can a dogaholic be?

Cough vs Coffin

Simon Want, vet

A vet colleague had a rather unfortunate incident when one of the two elderly owners of a small terrier dog had a heart attack in the consulting room. My friend was seemingly more worried about this than the owners. The old gentleman said, in a broad Glaswegian accent, "Don't worry about me, doc, just save my wee dog."

The dog had a mild bout of kennel cough.

After Henry

Di Holder, animal ambulance service

All dogs are special to their owners and mine are no exception. One in particular was just that little bit extra special. Without his love and devotion, I would not be leading a normal life now.

Henry, a Golden Retriever, came into my life in June 1988, when he was a 12-week-old bundle of fluff. When Henry arrived, I was suffering from severe agoraphobia, which is an extremely debilitating illness. I was housebound, too afraid to go out. A dog obviously needs to go out for walks and Henry was no exception. I knew that I needed to confront the outside world; it was up to me to make the effort to meet his needs. With his collar, lead and a 'poop' bag, Henry was ready to go, but was I?

We walked through the hallway. Henry was already used to wearing a collar and lead, as I had introduced them while in the house.

We approached the front door. Henry was full of confidence, but I was shaking from head to foot. When we actually reached the front door, it then took me at least 15 minutes to pluck up the courage to open it – the world beyond looked terrifying! I could not go on.

I looked down at my enthusiastic puppy ready for his first walk in the big, wide world. Those large brown eyes met mine and I knew I could not let him down. Even from such an early age (he was around 16 weeks old) he seemed to sense my inner terror and stayed close to my leg, giving it a gentle nudge. We slowly walked down the driveway to the pavement.

By this time, I felt mentally exhausted, my face dripping perspiration and my body full of fear. I could not move. Henry seemed to understand and he actually turned around and led me back to the front door.

Once inside, we both sat down, me shaking all over. He then jumped on my lap and gently licked my face. Those big, brown eyes said that he understood.

With Henry by my side, we gradually went further and further each day. It took more than a year, but, with his understanding and love, we eventually walked for miles even to the shops in the middle of our town.

Henry died at 15½ years of age. I lost the best friend

any human could have. For a while, I felt that my whole world had fallen apart, but I was determined not to let him down.

So, in Henry's memory, I started an animal ambulance service in 2001. Henry is still with me and I have photographs of him in the cab. Without his devotion and support, I would not be running the service or helping so many ill and injured animals.

I Want To Be Alone . . .

Viv Alemi, vet

Annie, a black Standard Poodle, was a very sensitive soul, and if voices were raised at home, she would leave the house and walk herself to the veterinary surgery, where she would sit quietly until her owners came to collect her.

Stand-up Comedy

Neil Allan former pet-food salesman

For many years, I worked for a very well-known pet-food company, and most of my time was spent setting up and managing the trade stand at dog shows throughout the UK and Europe. This was very hard work, and, obviously, targets had to be met. Therefore, like any good salesman I was always conscious of the need to project a good image to the public.

Every year, we would have a major campaign at Crufts Dog Show. Apart from promoting our products, it was a wonderful time to meet up with old friends, such as Guide Dogs' staff and clients.

A few years ago, I was well into the third day of Crufts, and business was very brisk. I was having a long discussion with some American visitors when an Irishman elbowed his way to the counter. He interrupted my flow by banging his fist and saying "Excuse me, but I need to discuss something with you urgently!"

I asked him to wait, as I was already dealing with someone. Again, he repeated his demands.

I asked the Americans if they would excuse me while I dealt with him. They happily agreed and stood to one side but remained in earshot.

"Now then," I said with as much patience as I could muster, "How can I help?"

"Well, you sold me a tin of that tripe yesterday. I gave it to my dog and he dropped down, stone dead!"

Oh no! My heart sank. The Americans edged forward, eager to hear the whole story.

The Irishman continued, "And then, I went to that rival food stand and they gave me some food. I fed it to my dog and he came back to life! By the way, let me introduce myself. Michael Edmondes, Irish Guide Dogs.

How are you?"

A wonderful wind up! Fortunately, the Americans saw the funny side and I made a good sale.

Despite my suspicions concerning the group behind it, I still support Guide Dogs with various fundraising events at the pub I now own.

Fete Worse Than Death

Neal King, vet and trustee of Guide Dogs

As the new boy in a rural veterinary practice, I was 'volunteered' to judge the dog show at the annual church fete.

I soon experienced the harsh reality of the single-handed challenge of announcing the next class, collecting the entries (and what passed for an entry fee), clearing a space on the vicarage lawn, marshalling the assorted entries, performing the charade of impartial judgement with the self-important dignity of the seasoned show judge, and finally announcing the result to the baleful glares of unplaced entrants.

The first lesson learnt was not to attempt to actually measure the tail of the German Shepherd in the Dog With The Longest Tail class. The most charitable interpretation of the subject's reaction was that it was loyally protecting its youthful owner from attack by a man with a stick. Alternatively, it was a downright neurotic of uncertain temperament. Either way, I am not that heroic and the attempt was a dismal failure, undermining all semblance of objectivity or scientific credibility in the judging. But I digress!

It is admitted, even by my most fervent admirers, that the afternoon deteriorated from shambles to farce. Near the end, we got to the Dog Most Like Owner class. Desperate for entrants, I was touting for custom among the milling masses when I came across a lady of advancing years in a tea-coloured Burberry raincoat and floppy hat.

She had once been ginger-headed but was now tea-coloured. She had freckles, which had faded to a tea colour. She was a study in drooping tea colour. Under her arm she had an ancient apricot Miniature Poodle with typically blocked tear ducts, another study in drooping tea colour. The likeness was staggering.

"Are you entering this class?" I enquired ingratiatingly, before blurting out, "You must be! You will win it hands down!"

Shaking her tea-coloured jowls vigorously, she pivoted on her green wellies and stomped off. The full enormity of my faux pas only became apparent to me when my agitated wife reported that none other than the 'Mrs Forbes Hamilton' of our village had been seen leaving the grounds, with her grandchildren prancing about her in high glee chanting, "Vet man says granny looks like the dog."